Plan and Section Drawing

Plan and Section Drawing
Second Edition

Thomas C. Wang

JOHN WILEY & SONS, INC.

New York   Chichester   Weinheim   Brisbane   Singapore   Toronto

This publication is designed to provide accurate and authoritative information in regard to the subject matter covered. It is sold with the understanding that the publisher is not engaged in rendering professional services. If professional advice or other expert assistance is required, the services of a competent professional person should be sought.

Library of Congress Cataloging-in-Publication Data:

Wang, Thomas C.
   Plan and section drawing/by Thomas C. Wang.—2nd ed.
      p.   cm.
   ISBN 0-471-28608-7
      1. Architectural drawing—Technique,   2. Architectural rendering—Technique.
3. Communication in architectural design—Technique.   I. Title.
NA2708.W36   1996   95-33704
720'.28'4—dc20

Printed in the United States of America

10   9

Dedication

To my wife Jacqueline and my sons Joseph, Andrew, and Matthew.

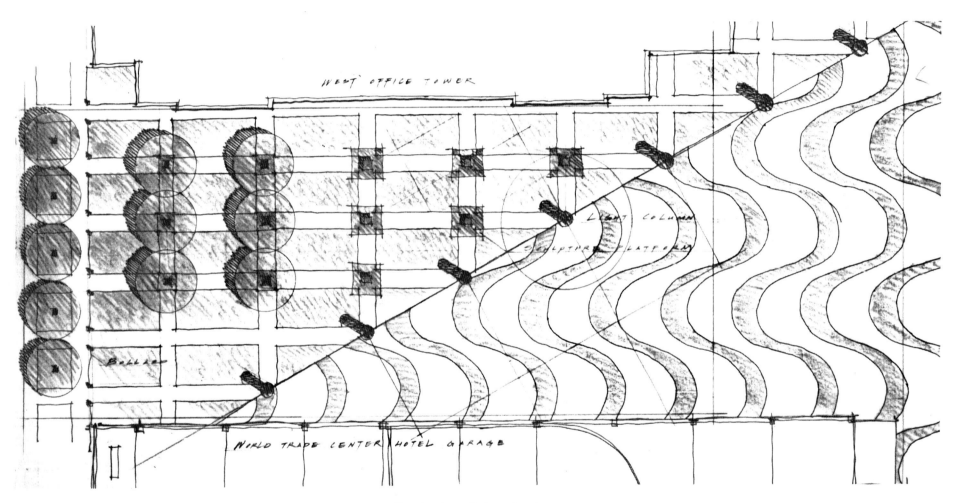

WEST OFFICE TOWER

LIGHT COLUMN

SCULPTURE PLATFORM

Bollard

WORLD TRADE CENTER HOTEL GARAGE

Drawing type: Schematic plan
Subject: Urban park
Medium/techniques: Uniball Micro and Prismacolor pencils on white tracing paper
Original size: 30" x 16"
Source: Wang Associates International

Contents

Credits

pages 14-17:   JJR Inc., Ann Arbor, Michigan

pages 20-21:   JJR Inc., Ann Arbor, Michigan

page 26:   JJR Inc., Ann Arbor, Michigan

pages 27-28:   Wang Associates International, Lincoln, Massachusetts

page 30:   Wang Associates International, Lincoln, Massachusetts (left and middle images); JJR Inc., Ann Arbor, Michigan (right image)

pages 33-34:   JJR Inc., Ann Arbor, Michigan

page 49:   EDAW Inc., Fort Collins, Colorado

page 50:   Student project, University of Michigan, Ann Arbor, Michigan

page 59:   Student project, University of Michigan, Ann Arbor, Michigan

page 67:   JJR Inc., Ann Arbor, Michigan

page 80:   JJR Inc., Ann Arbor, Michigan

page 82:   EDAW Inc., Fort Collins, Colorado (left image); JJR Inc., Ann Arbor, Michigan (right image)

page 83:   Student project, University of Michigan, Ann Arbor, Michigan

pages 86-87:   EDAW Inc., Fort Collins, Colorado

page 88:   Mitchell Nelson Welborn Reimann Partnership, Portland, Oregon (right image); JJR Inc., Ann Arbor, Michigan (left image)

page 90:   Mitchell Nelson Welborn Reimann Partnership, Portland, Oregon

page 99:   EDAW Inc., Fort Collins, Colorado

page 102:   EDAW Inc., Fort Collins, Colorado

page 117:   Student project, University of Michigan, Ann Arbor, Michigan

pages 120-122:   Student project, University of Michigan, Ann Arbor, Michigan

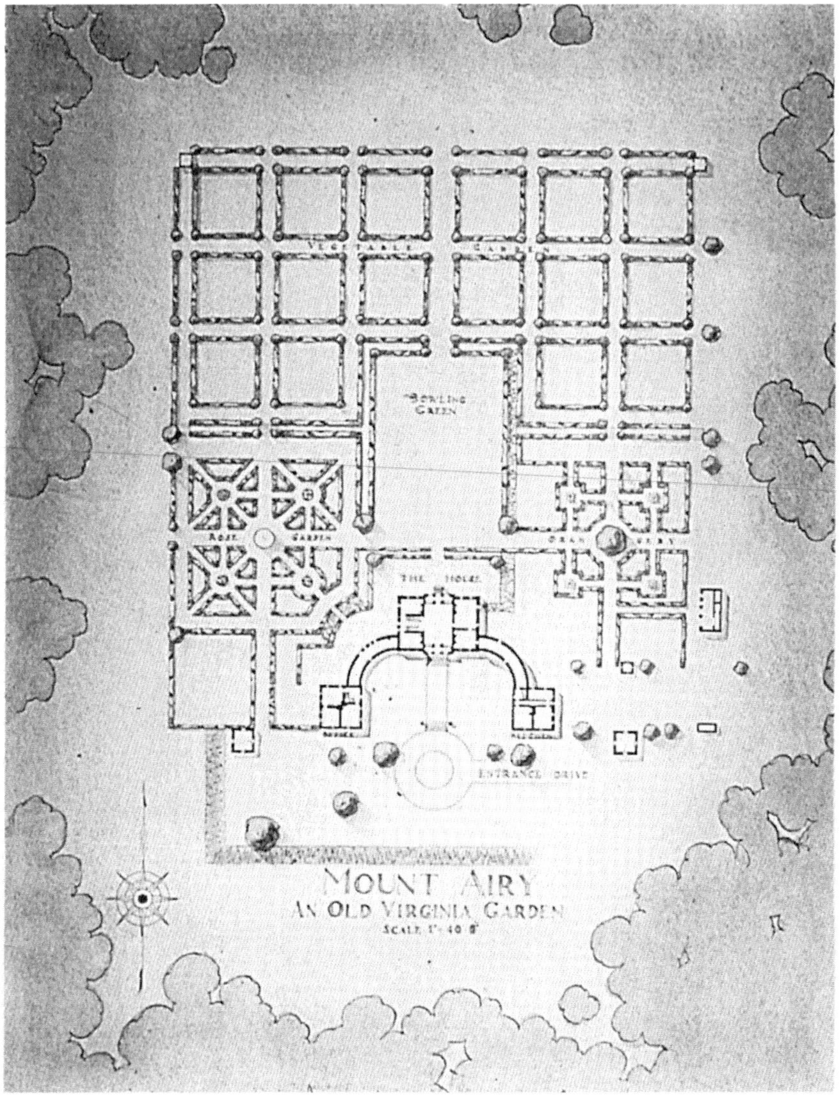

MOUNT AIRY
AN OLD VIRGINIA GARDEN
SCALE 1"=40'0"

Drawing type: Site plan
Subject: Historic drawing
Medium/techniques: Watercolor
Original size: 36" x 24"
Source: University of Illinois Department of Landscape Architecture Archive

Preface

The purpose of revising *Plan and Section Drawing* is to update the content and to make it more suitable to the needs of today's users and more in line with the thinking of contemporary graphic presentation. Although the pedagogical intent established 15 years ago remains valid and intact, most of the examples are in my opinion outdated. We have new ways of seeing and recording images. New media exist for graphic expressions. These changes are the result of advancement in the computer and copying industries which have introduced an entirely new spectrum of graphic communication products. Since the objective of this book is about the teaching of plan and section drawings within the larger context of design education, I believe that it is very important to incorporate these new communicational features in this new edition. This book is not intended to be a "graphic reference" comprised only of a collection of plan and section drawings. Instead this book emphasizes the "why this" and "how to" aspects of drawing plans and sections. In addition to discussing the basics on drawing skill, it is also my hope that this book can in its mysterious way instill the wisdom of choice in the making of graphic-related decisions. I hope that this book will continue to be a helpful guide to those who are beginning to communicate graphically.

Introduction

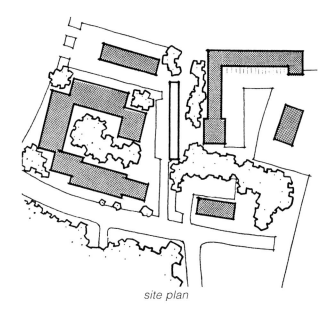

site plan

aerial photograph

Definition

Plan and section are the most common drawing types that designers use to communicate their design thoughts. Plan deals with the horizontal aspect and section deals with the vertical aspect of a design. They explain the design and serve as recording devices that document the evolution of the design process. Because design is a linear process of evolution, plan and section can and must take on a variety of appearances. Each and every one of these appearances is unique in its own graphic expression. For example, the loose doodlings and bubble diagrammings used at the beginning of a design process are very different from the carefully rendered and refined image of a master plan used for presentation to the clients. Each are intended for different sets of audiences and therefore have different missions. Different formats and expressions represent different stages of the design development. Yet despite the differences in appearance, these drawings are in principle interrelated because they grow with the design process and evolve from one drawing type to another. Within one project they share common site, scale, programs, and design intention. Therefore it is very important to understand the differences of these drawing types and to know the appropriate circumstances when using them.

Plan drawing is a kind of orthographic projection. It is very similar to aerial photographs, which not only show the horizontal distance between objects but also identify them.

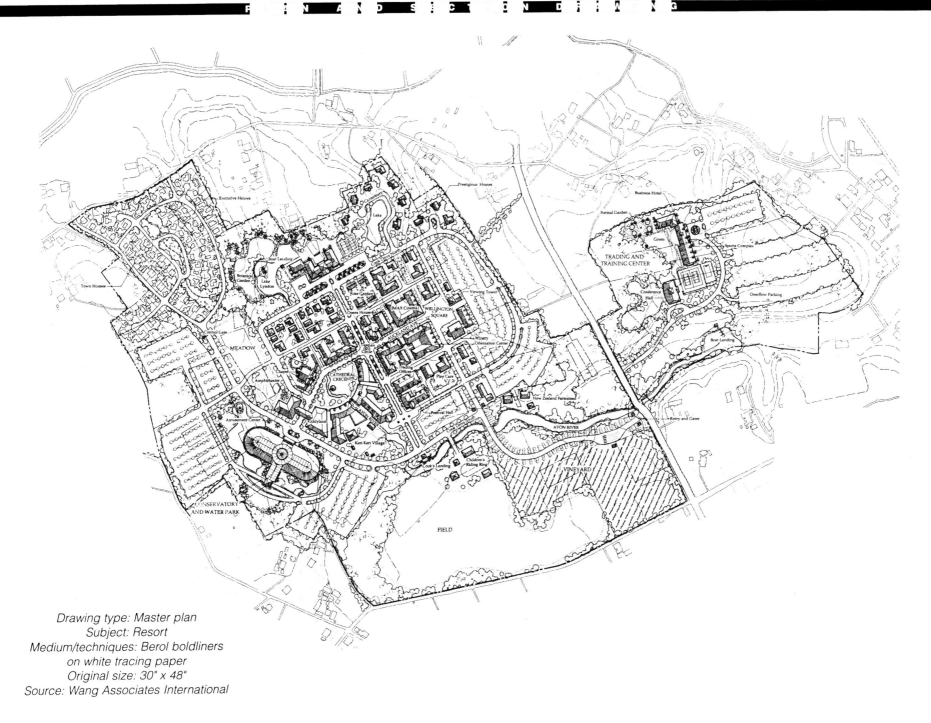

Drawing type: Master plan
Subject: Resort
Medium/techniques: Berol boldliners
on white tracing paper
Original size: 30" x 48"
Source: Wang Associates International

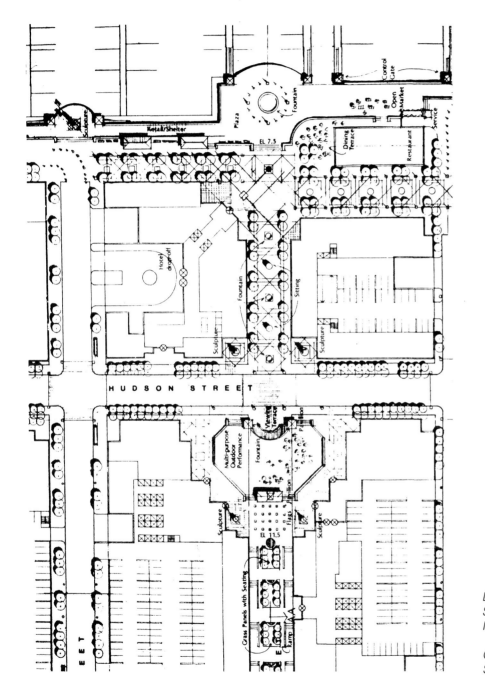

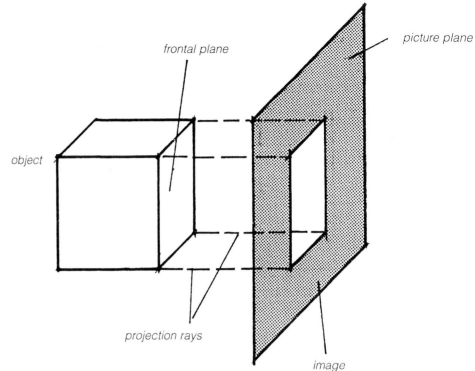

In orthographic projection the picture plane intercepts parallel projection rays from the frontal plane of the object. The projection rays are always perpendicular to the picture plane.

Drawing type: Site plan
Subject: Urban streetscape
Medium/techniques: Ink pen on
    white tracing paper
Original size: 48" x 30"
Source: Sasaki Associates Inc.

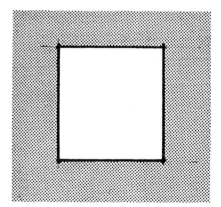

front view

front view

top view

side view

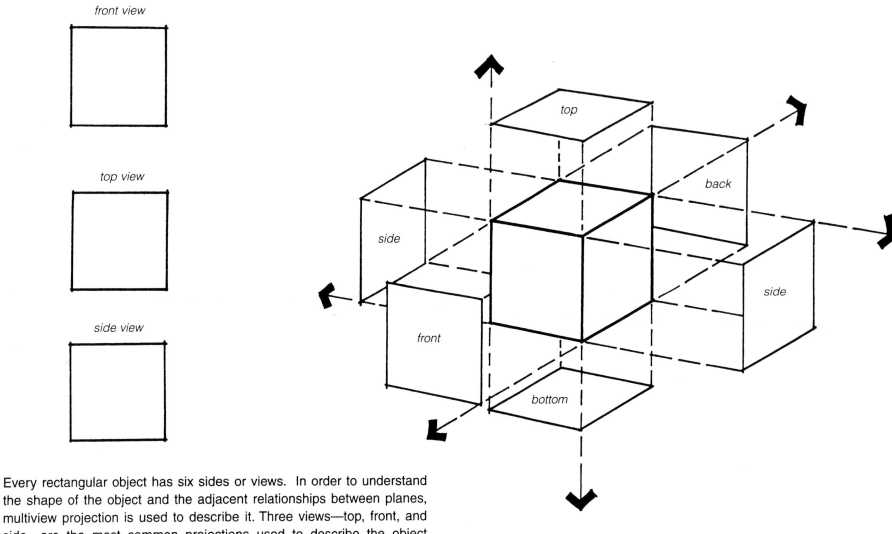

Every rectangular object has six sides or views. In order to understand the shape of the object and the adjacent relationships between planes, multiview projection is used to describe it. Three views—top, front, and side—are the most common projections used to describe the object graphically. Multiview projection is most often used in product design in which accurate measurement and exact image representation are required. In architecture and landscape architecture design, multiview projection is frequently used under different terminologies. A top view is the same as a plan; section and elevation are equivalent to a side view.

topographic map

building plan

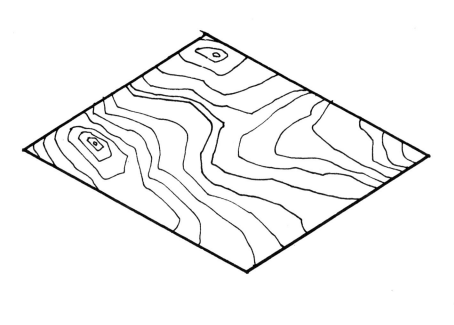

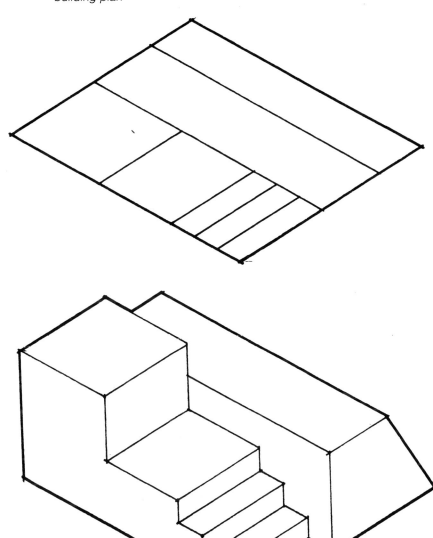

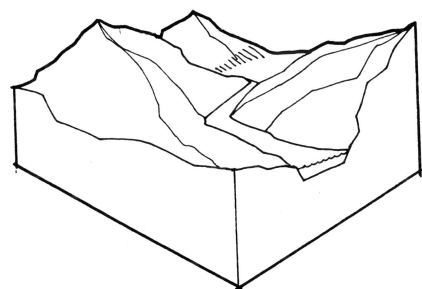

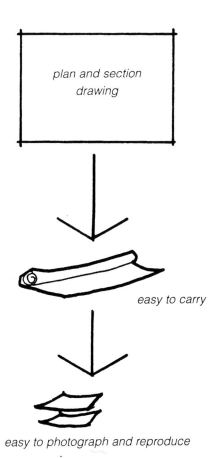

plan and section drawing

easy to carry

easy to photograph and reproduce

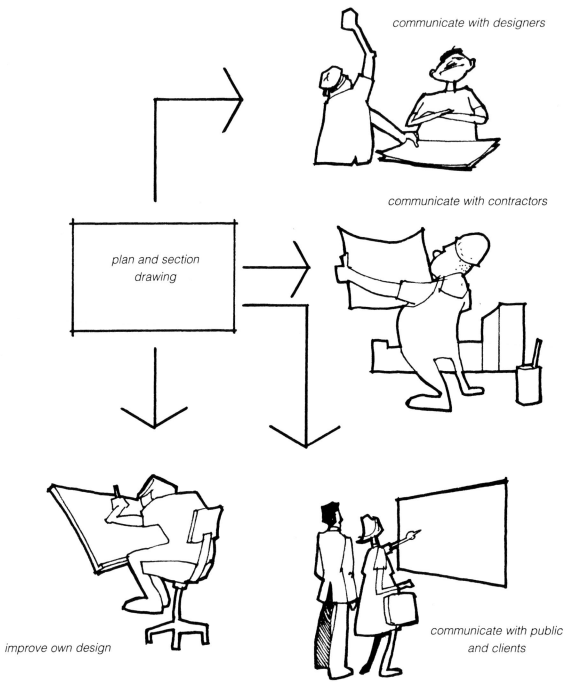

communicate with designers

communicate with contractors

plan and section drawing

improve own design

communicate with public and clients

Presentation Graphics vs. Process Graphics

My biggest frustration in the many years of teaching design and graphics is that students are often only interested in the so-called "presentation graphics." The teaching of graphics becomes the teaching of making fancy drawings for presentation. The reasons for the preference are all too obvious. According to the students' perceptions, nicely drawn plans and sections sell. There is no ground to suggest that nice graphics mean good design, but the general consensus is that good design is often accompanied by good graphics. Attempts to teach "process graphics" often fail miserably because process graphics consists of a documentary of individualized and personal experience. These codified individual messages are very difficult to transplant from one designer to another.

The truth of the matter is that there is no clear distinction between "process" and "presentation" graphic materials. The drawing type may vary due to purposes and audience. Amount of detail and style of expression may differ as ideas are developed over time. Keep in mind that the notion of "presentation" is artificial and driven by due dates. Any drawings accomplished along this design process should be able to serve as presentation purposes at anytime when called for. As long as drawings are done in the same scales and "attentiveness," any drawings, plans, or sections can be used for making a presentation. These are called the "progress drawings."

Unfortunately due dates in the academic environment historically demanded a more carefully drawn set of drawings. This good intention originated as a device to add a touch of formality to the presentation has grown into a big deal. Such excessive attention has been paid to the preparation of the presentation "package" that the thinking process and the quality of design are compromised. Of course one could argue that presentation is part of the design process and that one should carefully package the presentational materials as part of the show. Indeed the argument is true because this is exactly what is being done in the real world. Presentations require major investment of money and time. The presentation can also make or break a project. Students should be exposed to a variety of presentation graphics and be taught the technical aspect of how to prepare them. They should be aware of the cost and benefit of these techniques and be able to make wise decisions in their academic and professional life.

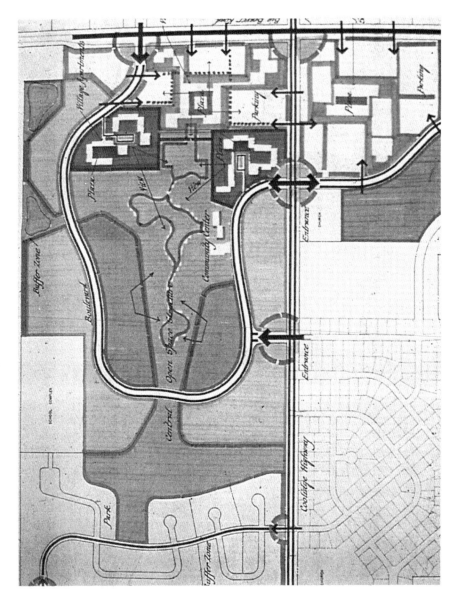
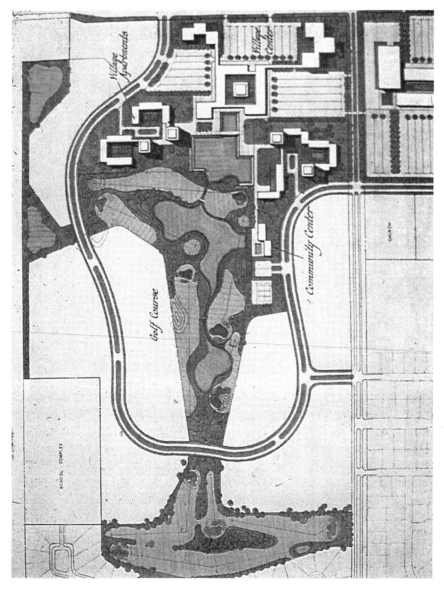

Drawing type: Schematic site plan
Subject: Golf community
Medium/techniques: Markers on blackline print
Original size: 36" x 24"
Source: JJR Inc.

Pages 9, 10, 11, & 12:
Drawing type: Conceptual plan, master plan,
site plan, and section/elevation
Subject: Institutional planning
Medium/techniques: Pilot razor point on white
tracing paper
Original size: 34" x 48"
Source: Wang Associates International

LEGEND

1 UNIVERSAL HOUSE
2 HOUSE FOR HUMAN RIGHTS
3 ACADEMIC INSTITUTE
4 COURT
5 ATHIR LIBRARY
6 DIAMOND COLLEGE (TWIN LOCATION)
7 HOTEL (W/ PARKING BELOW)
8 HOTEL PARLIAMENT/OFFICE UNION
9 FIELD OF DIGNITY (W/ SPORT PAVILION)
10 MULTI-FUNCTIONAL AREA (GROUND FLOOR ONLY)
11 TENNIS CLUB
12 PARKING FOR VISITORS (BELOW + W/)
13 PARKING FOR RIGHT FLAT FUNCTION (HO)
14 PARKING FOR UNO (UNDERGROUND)
15 REMOTE SERVICE AREA (ADD W/ NATION)

CONCEPTUAL MASTER PLAN

PLACE DES NATION

1 : 2500

Existing Figure/Ground (Buildings)

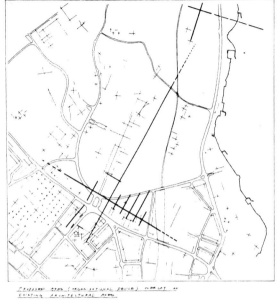

Proposed Grids (Organizational Device) Overlay on
Existing Architectural Axes

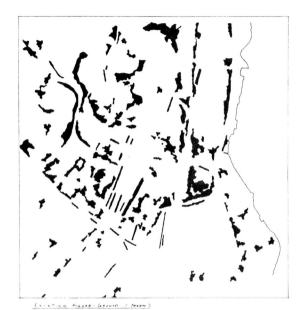

(Existing Figure/Ground (Trees)

Proposed Figure/Ground (Buildings)

Proposed Figure/Ground (Trees)

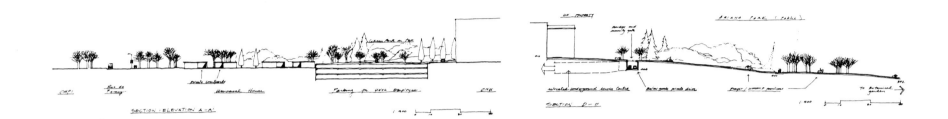

SECTION - ELEVATION A-A'

SECTION D-D

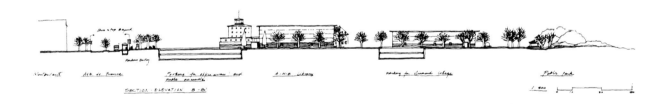

SECTION - ELEVATION B-B'

ELEVATION C-C'

Design Process

A normal design process traditionally includes preliminary design (conceptual design), schematic design, design development, construction documents, bidding, and construction supervision. Plans and sections of various forms are used extensively in all of these steps with perhaps the exception of bidding.

Preliminary design includes site inventory and analysis, background research, and analysis of the development program. Landscape characters are analyzed according to their development potential and suitability. Values are assigned to these landscape characters according to their relative importance within the hierarchy of a specific program. Preliminary design also includes concept formulation and development. Design concepts are generated, tested, and evaluated independently as well as tested according to the opportunities and constraints of the landscape characteristics.

Schematic design verifies the confirmed concept and refines the preliminary design. Schematic design takes place over these functional diagrams and particularly evolves from the original land-use diagram. As scale and proportion become more real and accurate, design intent and consciousness likewise become more focused. The design program often becomes more realistic and fixed and by now, one should gain a better understanding of dimensions and sizes of each of the components required. It is at this point that familiar and realistic images such as buildings and tree massing begin to reveal themselves through layers of tracing paper. At the same time sections and elevations are cut to better understand the vertical relationship between all the design components. In essence this is design.

Design development is the stage when the design has finally received initial approval. The concept is sold and the initial design articulation seems to make sense. It is at this point when more detailed design investigations are required to verify the decisions as well as the exploration of design alternatives. For example, a brick-paved plaza approved at the schematic design must now require a more thorough investigation of paving pattern and drainage. Perhaps the plaza is on a raised deck and the spacing of large trees and water features must relate to the structural columns supporting the deck from underneath. Detail plans and sections are therefore critical in making these design decisions. Often Computer-Aided Drafting and Design (CADD) is used because of the demand for accuracy as well as the ease of modification. Color and fancy graphics are no longer important because the purposes are different.

Construction documents are graphic conclusions of the design process. These drawings accurately describe the design in detail including the listing of all dimensions, materials, methods of construction, and finishes. Plans and sections drawn at large scale are used to communicate information to the builders and contractors. Pricing and construction costs are determined based on the information given on these documents. Construction Documents (CDs) are also binding legal documents between the clients, architects, and contractors. Fancy and colorful graphics are nonessential in expressing these documents. Accuracy and clarity are the most important criteria.

In order to anticipate unexpected changes, construction documents must be highly flexible and relatively inexpensive to revise. To accommodate minor changes and to avoid redrawing the entire sheet of document, CADD has been the indispensable device in the preparation of construction documents. They are highly accurate and can be easily prepared and modified. CDs prepared by CADD are the standard expectation in design industry and today's clients expect nothing less. Furthermore, Geodetic Index Survey (GIS) data and other chartered surveying information on disc are readily available in the preparation of base information. There is no reason not to use CADD from the very beginning so that all the analytical and design work can be done on an accurate and consistent base throughout the entire design process.

Regional Maps

Regional maps are maps that show the entire region.

There are many different types of plan drawing, and each has its own purpose. The following illustrations demonstrate the use of different types of plan drawings in a typical design process.

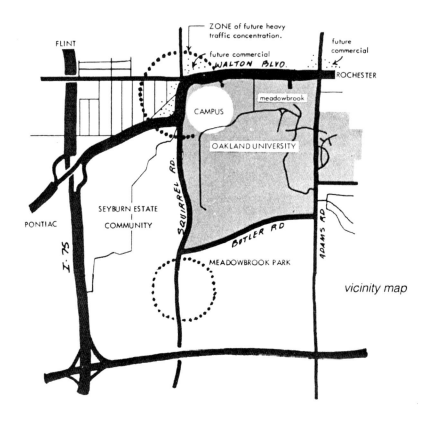

vicinity map

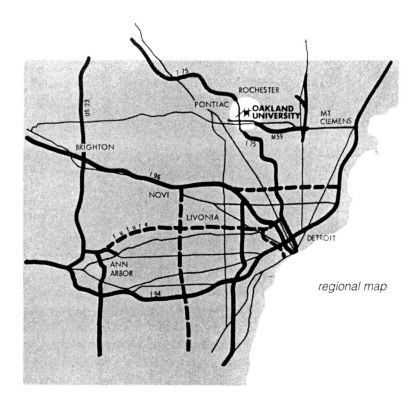

regional map

Vicinity Maps

Vicinity maps are maps that show the adjacent land uses that surround the study area. It usually covers the same watershed or township or is bounded by the major road system.

Site-Information Maps

Site-information maps are maps that contain necessary background information about the site. This data is often available from sources such as the Soil Survey or Public Works Department. Data maps frequently used by environmental designers are the soil map, land-use map, and vegetation map.

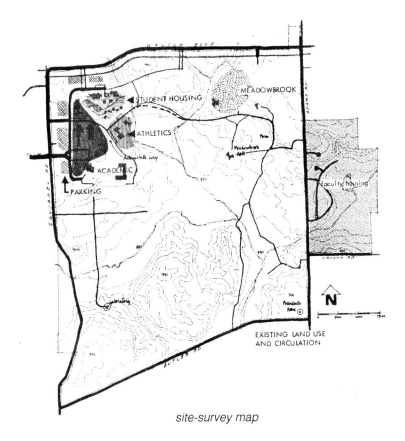

site-survey map

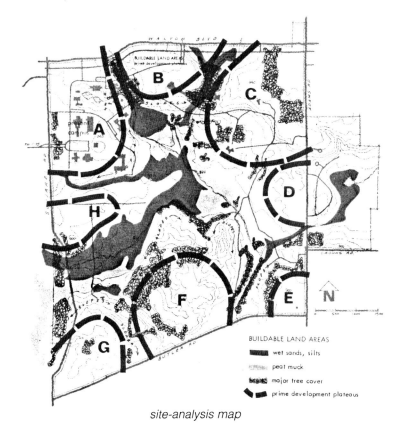

site-analysis map

conceptual layout maps

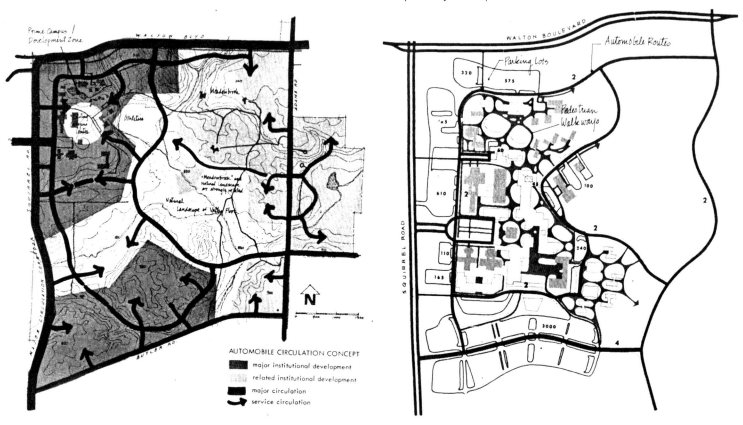

AUTOMOBILE CIRCULATION CONCEPT

■ major institutional development
▨ related institutional development
▬ major circulation
↝ service circulation

conceptual diagrams

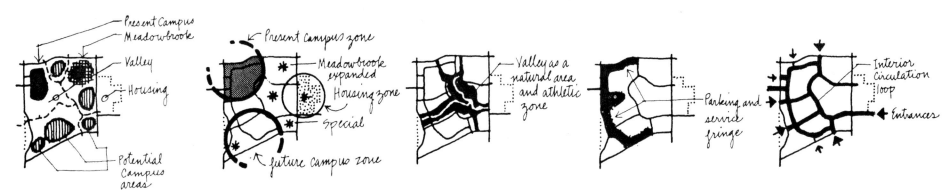

master plan and perspective

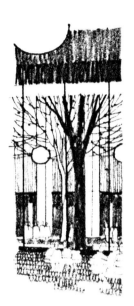

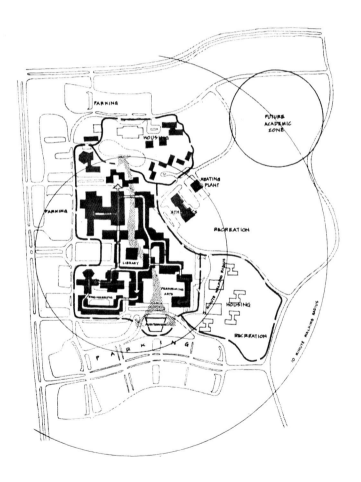

Analytical Drawings

Analytical drawings are one of the most important drawing types in a typical design process. Site analysis includes site inventory—a process that records the existing site conditions and graphically represents them according to the needs of the design program and intention. Typically, existing site data includes physical or natural information such as soil, vegetation, slope surface water, ground water bedrock, and many others. Political and socioeconomic data are also important and they may include property boundaries, land uses, transportation system and traffic conditions, and historical features as well as many others. Minimum site data normally includes a survey map delineating all property lines, and a topographical base map showing site contours and geographical features.

If necessary, each of the site data can be further subdivided into subsects according to the needs of the development program. For example, a more detailed breakdown of the slope condition is required to locate housing development on a hillside. Information on bedrock and depth must be carefully charted when dredging and excavation are required. Much of this information is readily available from the Soil Survey or Public Works Department. Other sources include GIS and satellite or aerial photographs. Of course, the easiest way to record this information on a small site is by actual field reconnaissance.

Site analysis weighs each piece of the site data according to the design criteria and compares them with other data to determine their degree of importance within a specific design problem. This prioritizing process establishes a decision-making hierarchy that enables the designer to plan intelligently, logically, and be environmentally sensitive to the land. Land suitability and development feasibility can be quickly determined and vulnerability avoided. In essence, site analysis drawings allow the designer to visually grasp these concerns and be able to pinpoint the opportunities and constraints of the land.

A synthesis diagram is a map or an overlay that summarizes the result of the analytical process. It not only summarizes the opportunities and constraints of the land based on the understanding of the development criteria, but at the same time, begins making general design assumptions. These assumptions can be as specific as the preferred location of a house, pool, driveway, and so on. It can also be expressed as a development strategy such as indicating a preferred land-use allocation pattern or demarcating a land conservation district. It is at this particular juncture of the design process that design intuition and creativity begin to take over from the mundane fact-finding mission.

Analytical drawings are often expressed in plans because of the format which data is traditionally recorded. Depending on the scale, maps can cover a relatively large area and contain plenty of information. Section, on the other hand, cannot offer similar coverage as that of a plan but it can supplement the plan with vertical information especially when dealing with slope, soil, and other geological data. Because the grand mission of analytical drawings is to inform, such drawings are often color coded to highlight their messages. For example, boldness of lines is used to describe the various levels of use intensity in a circulation diagram. Arrows and circular and star-shaped symbols are incorporated to indicate linkages and important nodes. Different shades of colors are used to express the steepness of slope. In addition, generous annotations will help clarify the information and demystify the abstractness.

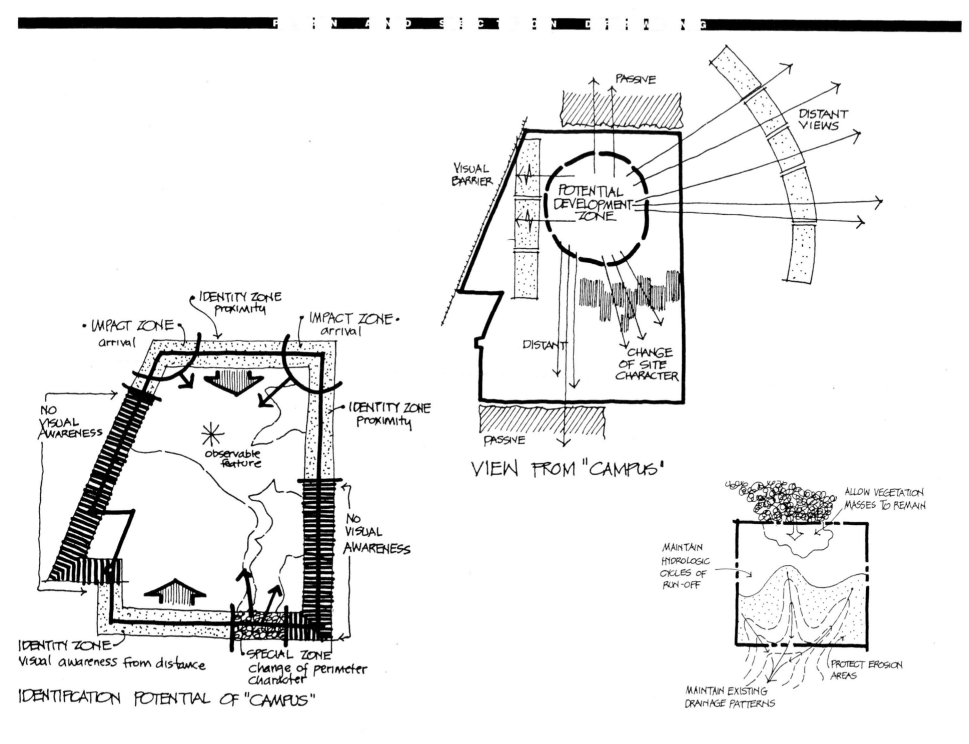

VISUAL BARRIER

PASSIVE

DISTANT VIEWS

POTENTIAL DEVELOPMENT ZONE

DISTANT

CHANGE OF SITE CHARACTER

PASSIVE

VIEW FROM "CAMPUS"

• IMPACT ZONE • arrival

IDENTITY ZONE proximity

IMPACT ZONE • arrival

NO VISUAL AWARENESS

IDENTITY ZONE Proximity

✴ observable feature

NO VISUAL AWARENESS

IDENTITY ZONE Visual awareness from distance

SPECIAL ZONE change of perimeter character

IDENTIFICATION POTENTIAL OF "CAMPUS"

ALLOW VEGETATION MASSES TO REMAIN

MAINTAIN HYDROLOGIC CYCLES OF RUN-OFF

PROTECT EROSION AREAS

MAINTAIN EXISTING DRAINAGE PATTERNS

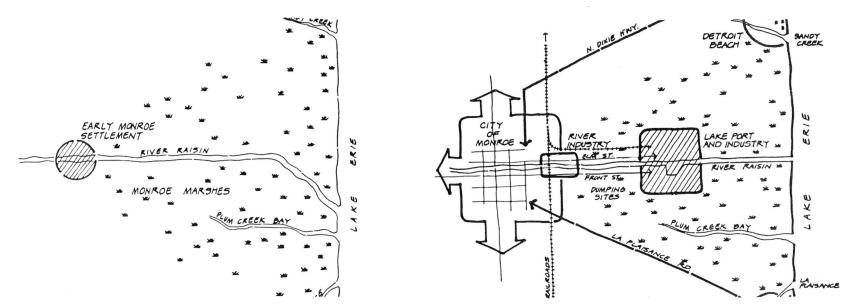

Drawing type: Site analysis plans
Subject: City planning
Medium/techniques: Felt tip markers
Original size: 8 1/2" x 11"
Source: JJR Inc.

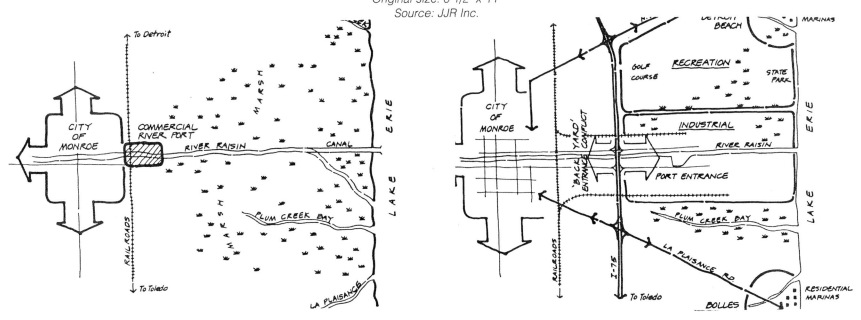

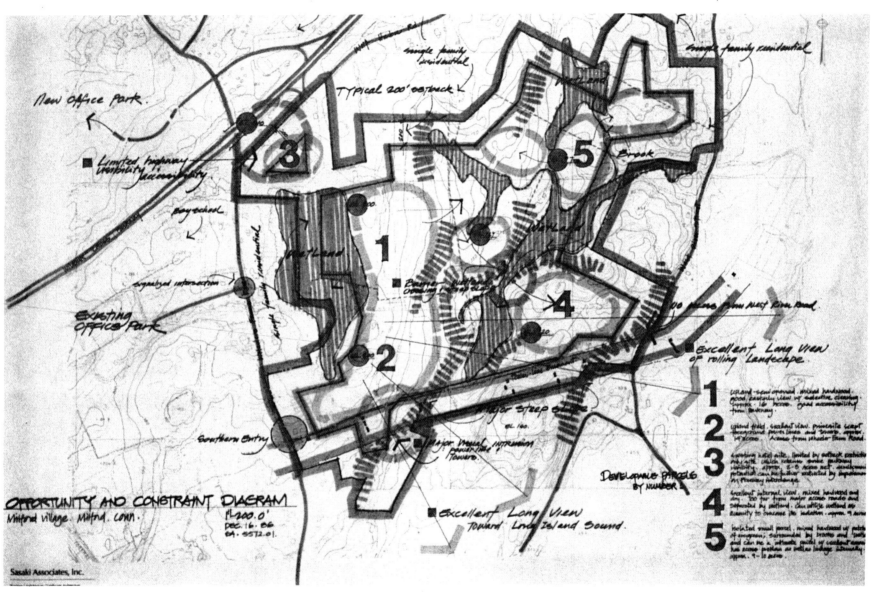

Drawing type: Site synthesis plan
Subject: Office park
Medium/techniques: Markers on blackline print
Original size: 36" x 24"
Source: Sasaki Associates Inc.

Changes in VISUAL CONE.

peripheral cone of pedestrian

peripheral cone of vision for motorist.

pedestrian cone of vision

motorist cone of vision

(A) lane management.
(B) transit mall.

auto-domain

pedestrian territory.

p. cone.

cone of vision

d: distance between viewers & shop windows

OLD sidewalk

new curb

BUS   BUS

cone of vision (pedestrian.)

"decorative pavement."

Bus shelter.

curbs kiosk etc...

Bldg

wall   ceiling (roof)

existing wall: Bldg. facade.

HORIZON

FLOOR

* it creates 3 new compartments

Drawing type: Sections
Subject: Streetscape analysis
Medium/techniques: Berol boldliners on white paper
Original size: 8 1/2" x 11"
Source: Wang Associates International

Concept Drawings

Conceptual drawings are embryonic design diagrams. These diagrams vary from little thumbnail sketches on yellow note pads to doodlings on dinner napkins to scribbles on tracing paper. They often begin without specific scale and reference of orientation. They begin with simple and abstract graphic notations of lines and symbols and slowly evolve into tangible images that meet the design program. Because concept formulation and development deal with the growth of a design idea, conceptual drawings therefore bear the personality and characteristic of each designer. These drawings are unique and special because of their individualized format and expression.

There are no standard graphic conventions in conceptual drawings. Content of these conceptual drawings is in principle the graphic equivalent of spoken words. By way of composition, this graphic vocabulary tracks the individual designer's thinking process. Idea tracking by diagramming is the most effective way to visualize the "design thoughts" and the best way to record the thought process. The simplicity and fluidity of the line and the dynamic of the expression are very powerful messages indeed. However, we must recognize that there are many steps in between these seductive dinner napkin images and the final products. The logic of progression between ideation and the evolution of ideas should not be ignored or treated as a mystery that only happens inside the "black box." In reality, every step of the design process is traceable and defensible. There is logic in every step taken and each must be clearly understood. In short, there is no giant leap between ideation and final realiza-

tion. An attempt to leap without diligently following each step is bound to lead to failure.

These steps are represented by a series of plans and sections done at a prescribed scale so the designer can visually interact with them, understand them, and ultimately improve them. This repetitive drawing effort on tracing paper or on any kind of semitransparent material allows design ideas to filter and permeate through the layers. These overlays serve as the forum for design critique and a springboard for the better design to come. The two most important purposes of analytical diagrams in a design process are "self-critique" and peer communication.

Concept diagrams are usually expressed in plans but can also be expressed as three-dimensional sketches. The evolution of these diagrams quickly finds them attached to a site synthesis plan and it is at this point that scale becomes an issue. Further development of these conceptual diagrams—or bubbles—will lead to the breakup of the bubble into various functional diagrams each of which carries a specific message. Common functional diagrams include land use and space allocation, vehicular and pedestrian circulation, public and private open spaces, and so on. Functional diagrams are usually drawn in the same scale as the analytical plans—or master plan—and can be expressed independently as well as serve as layers of overlays on top of the master plan. Again the important thing to remember is simplicity and clarity of the messages. Focus should be on quality and not quantity.

Bubble Diagrams

These diagrammatic drawings are very important in concept development during the design process. They are the graphic shorthand that records the designer's thought process and the ideas that are generated. These diagrams are highly abstract and symbolic. Written descriptions are needed to help others to understand.

bubble diagram

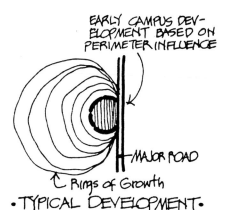
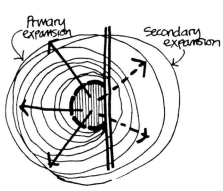
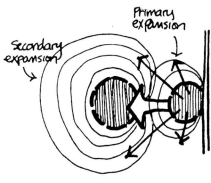
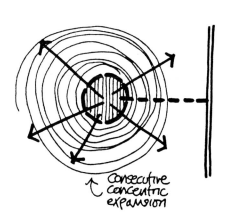

evolution of bubble diagram

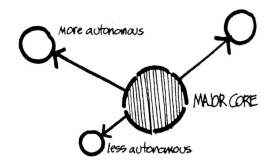
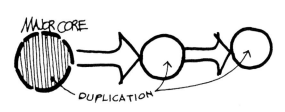
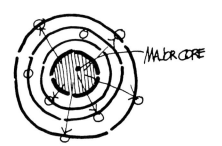

Conceptual Diagrams

Conceptual diagrams are derived directly from bubble diagrams. They are highly abstract and symbolic.

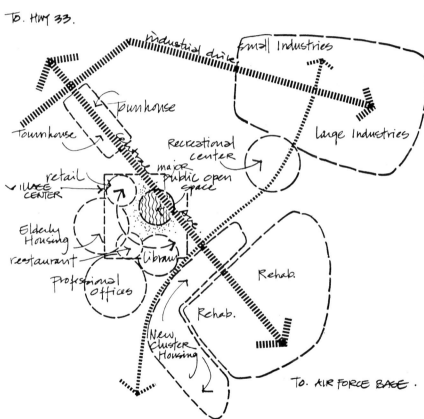

CONCEPT ORGANIZATION DIAGRAM

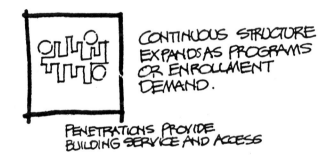

CONTINUOUS STRUCTURE EXPANDS AS PROGRAMS OR ENROLLMENT DEMAND.

PENETRATIONS PROVIDE BUILDING SERVICE AND ACCESS

27

"ORIGINAL CONCEPT"

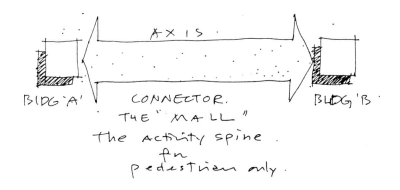

AXIS

BLDG 'A'   CONNECTOR.   BLDG 'B'
                  THE "MALL"
                  the activity spine.
                  for
                  pedestrian only.

"MODIFIED CONCEPT II"

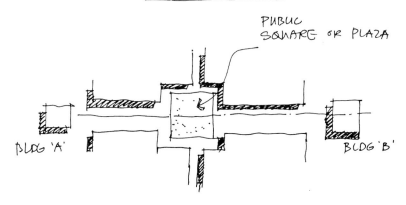

PUBLIC
SQUARE OR PLAZA

BLDG 'A'   BLDG 'B'

"MODIFIED CONCEPT"

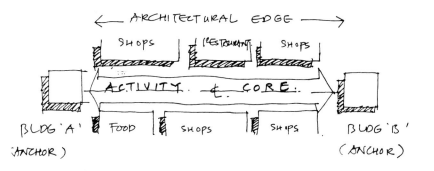

← ARCHITECTURAL EDGE →

SHOPS   RESTAURANT   SHOPS

ACTIVITY . & . CORE .

BLDG 'A'   FOOD   SHOPS   SHIPS   BLDG 'B'
(ANCHOR)   (ANCHOR)

(VILLAGE SQUARE CONCEPT)   CONCEPT-1

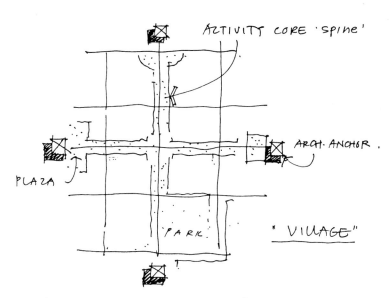

ACTIVITY CORE 'Spine'

ARCH. ANCHOR .

PLAZA

PARK   "VILLAGE"

(VILLAGE SQUARE CONCEPT)   CONCEPT - 2

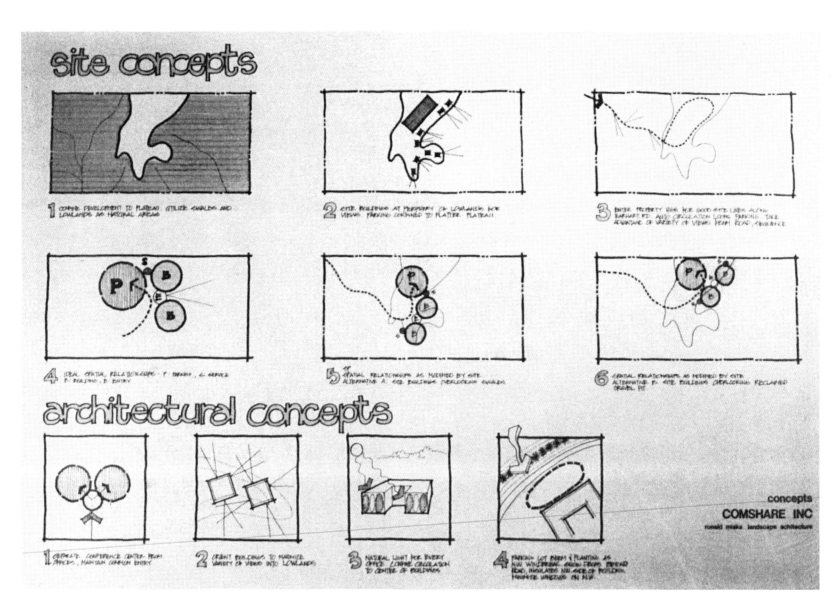

Drawing type: Concept diagrams
Subject: Landscape designs
Medium/techniques: Pentel signpen on white paper
Original size: 42" x 30"
Source: Student work, University of Michigan

Conceptual Maps

In conceptual maps the refined concept is drawn on top of the base map. Concepts can therefore be site-specific.

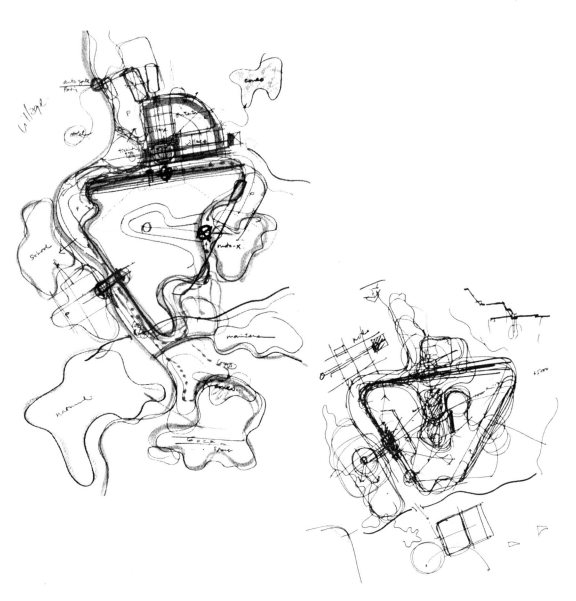

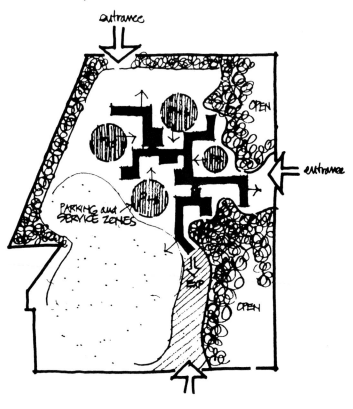

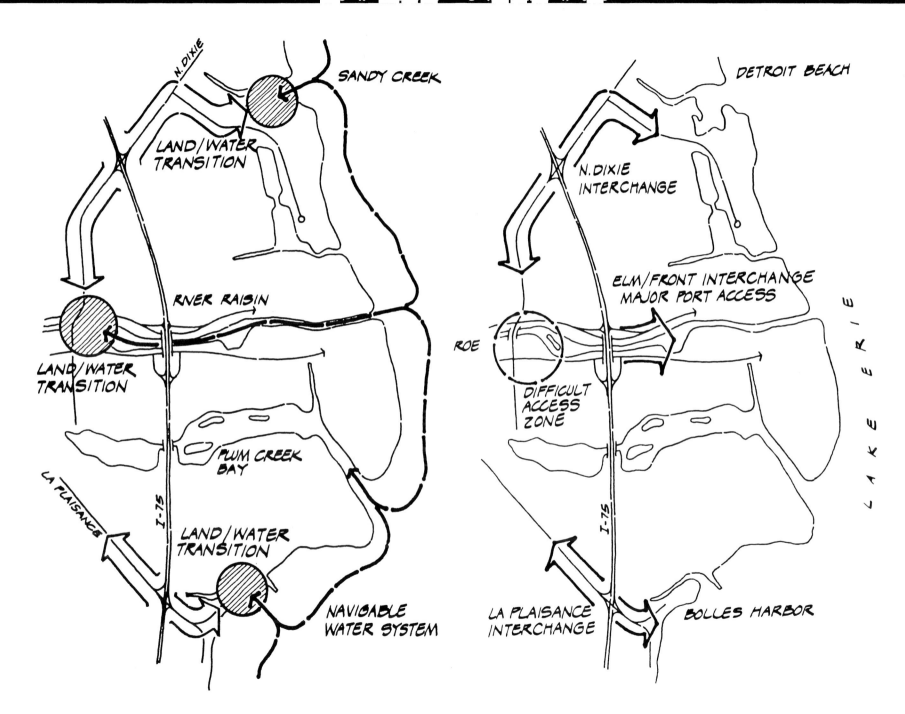

SANDY CREEK

N. DIXIE

LAND/WATER
TRANSITION

RIVER RAISIN

LAND/WATER
TRANSITION

LA PLAISANCE

I-75

PLUM CREEK
BAY

LAND/WATER
TRANSITION

NAVIGABLE
WATER SYSTEM

DETROIT BEACH

N. DIXIE
INTERCHANGE

ELM/FRONT INTERCHANGE
MAJOR PORT ACCESS

ROE

DIFFICULT
ACCESS
ZONE

LAKE ERIE

I-75

LA PLAISANCE
INTERCHANGE

BOLLES HARBOR

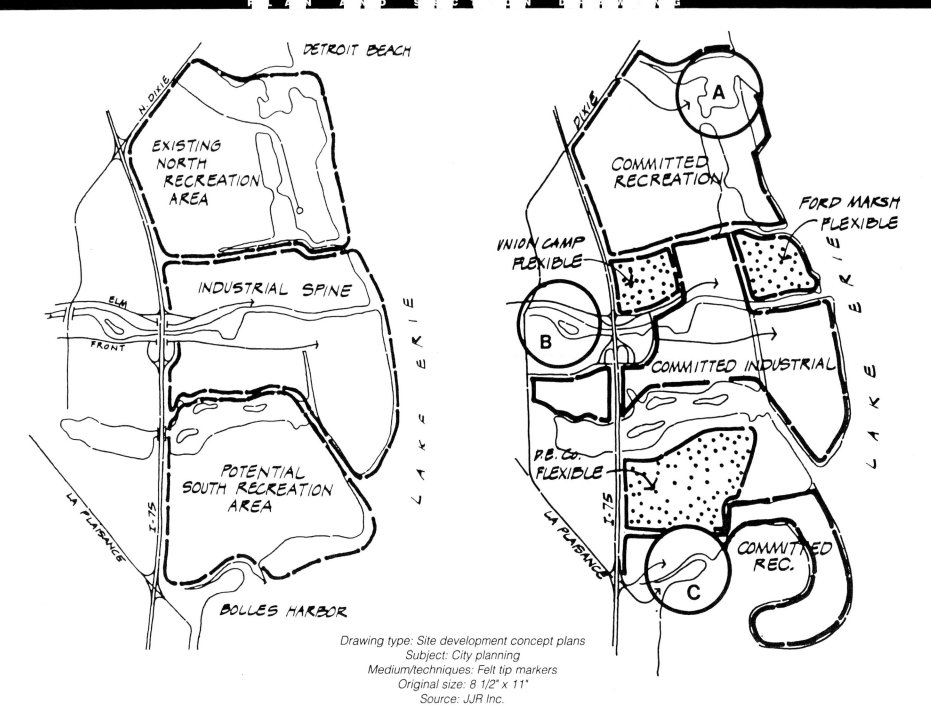

DETROIT BEACH

N. DIXIE

EXISTING
NORTH
RECREATION
AREA

INDUSTRIAL SPINE

ELM

FRONT

POTENTIAL
SOUTH RECREATION
AREA

LA PLAISANCE

I-75

BOLLES HARBOR

LAKE ERIE

DIXIE

COMMITTED
RECREATION

A

UNION CAMP
FLEXIBLE

FORD MARSH
FLEXIBLE

B

COMMITTED INDUSTRIAL

D.E. CO.
FLEXIBLE

C

COMMITTED
REC.

LA PLAISANCE

I-75

LAKE ERIE

Drawing type: Site development concept plans
Subject: City planning
Medium/techniques: Felt tip markers
Original size: 8 1/2" x 11"
Source: JJR Inc.

Design Drawings

6

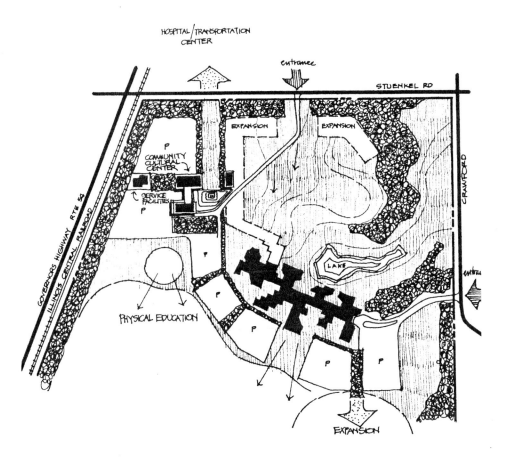

Design drawings are drawings that document the progress of the design development phase. They include plans and sections as well as perspectives and models. There are no time limits on the length of this phase other than an arbitrary dateline established by individuals such as clients or teachers. Likewise, there are no limits on the type of drawings one should include in design development. A designer does not produce one set of plans and sections at the end of the design development phase. A designer begins with plans and sections and continues to refine and reproduce them as time allows.

As described earlier in this book, the most important purpose for a designer to draw is self-communication. A designer must be able to visualize his or her design by drawing it. Drawings stimulate visual and mental responses and invite changes. Changes in design are redrawn and reviewed, and the cycle of self-communication continues. Discussion with peers or presentation to clients is also part of the design development process. As time goes, design becomes more mature and precise and the design message becomes more concrete. Plans and sections therefore become more informative and legible.

Final Site-Development Plan

This is also called the master plan. It shows the final design solution and includes building masses, road layouts, planting schemes, and the location of all design elements. Depending on the nature of the design project, the format of the master plan varies from a detailed precise document to a general schematic layout.

Preliminary-Design Maps

The following four examples illustrate the birth of a design solution. It evolved on different layers of tracing paper. Design ideas are recorded on tracing paper, and design concepts and objectives are tested and compared. A solution is eventually evolved and finalized so that it satisfies most of the requirements.

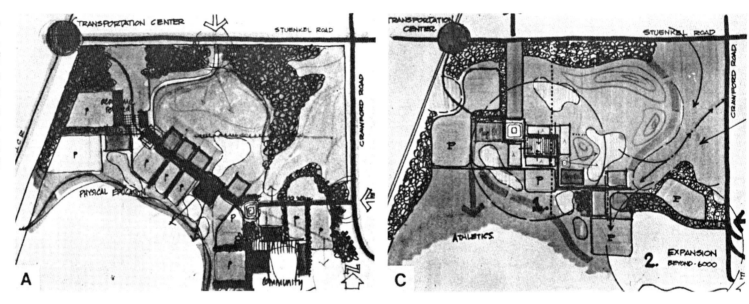

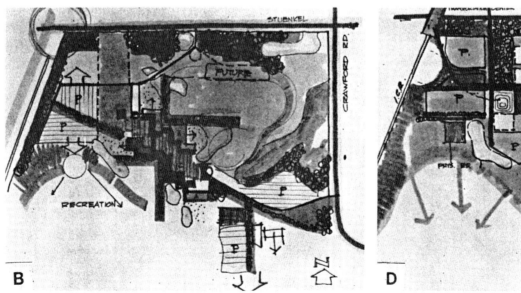

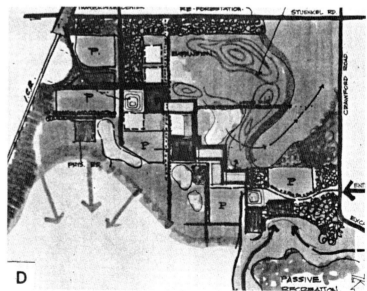

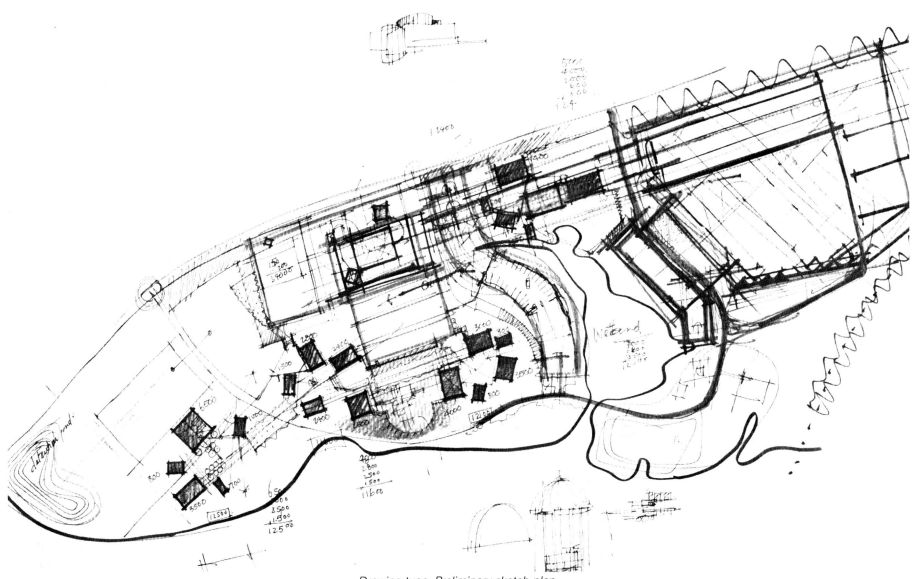

Drawing type: Preliminary sketch plan
Subject: Shopping center
Medium/techniques: Felt tip markers, Berol boldliner, and colored pencils
Original size: 24" x 36"
Source: Wang Associates International

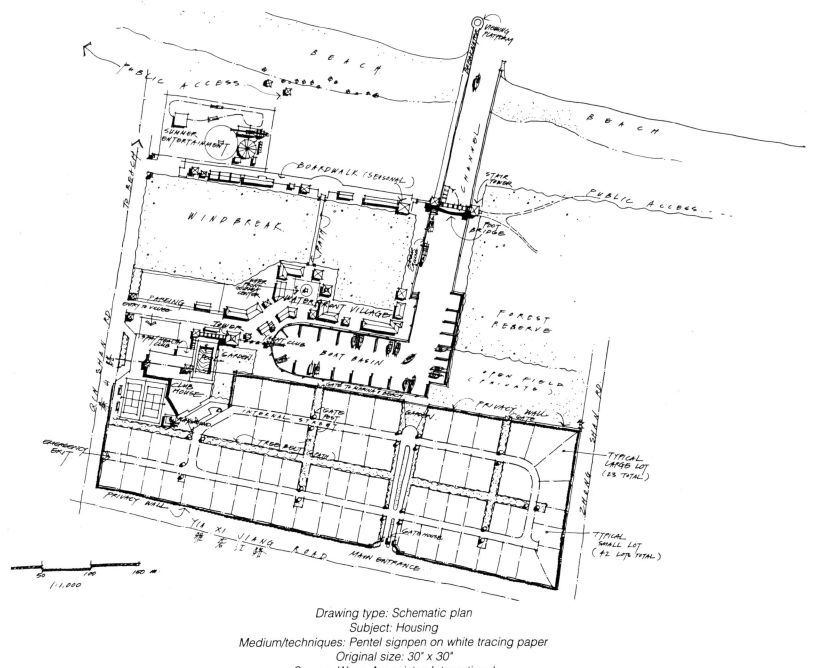

Drawing type: Schematic plan
Subject: Housing
Medium/techniques: Pentel signpen on white tracing paper
Original size: 30" x 30"
Source: Wang Associates International

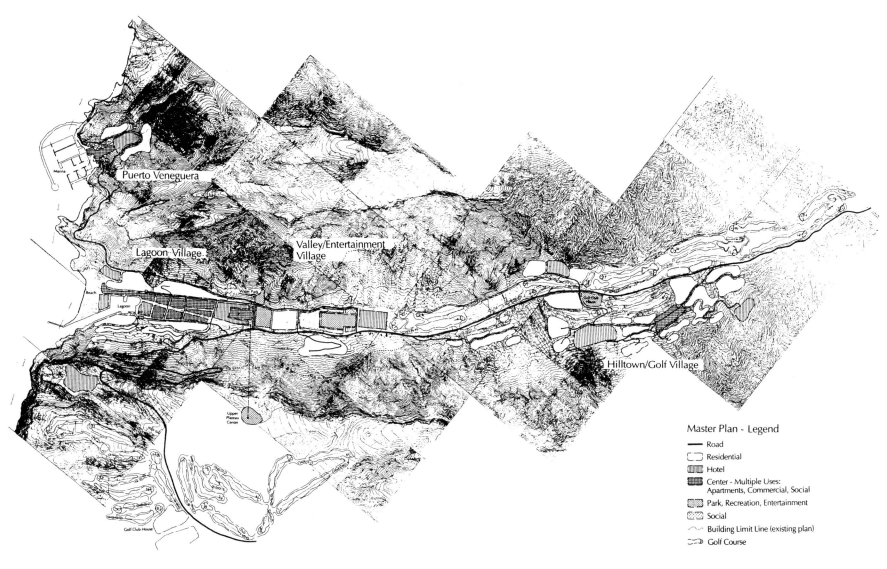

Puerto Veneguera

Lagoon Village

Valley/Entertainment Village

Hilltown/Golf Village

Marina

Beach

Lagoon

Water Park

Upper Plateau Center

Golf Club House

Master Plan - Legend

— Road
⸦‾⸧ Residential
▥ Hotel
▦ Center - Multiple Uses: Apartments, Commercial, Social
▨ Park, Recreation, Entertainment
▦ Social
↝ Building Limit Line (existing plan)
⊏⊐ Golf Course

Pages 37, 38, & 39:
Drawing type: Plan/section/elevation
Subject: Resort planning
Medium/techniques: Berol boldliner on white tracing paper
Original size: plan: 30" x 56"; section: 30" x 48"; elevation: 30" x 48"
Source: Sasaki Associates Inc.

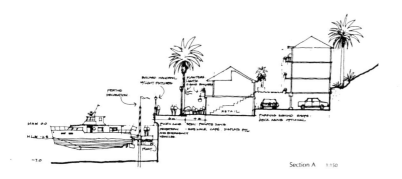

Section A 1:150

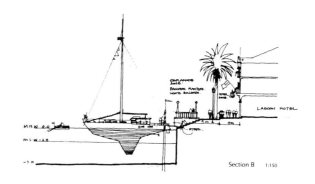

Section B 1:150

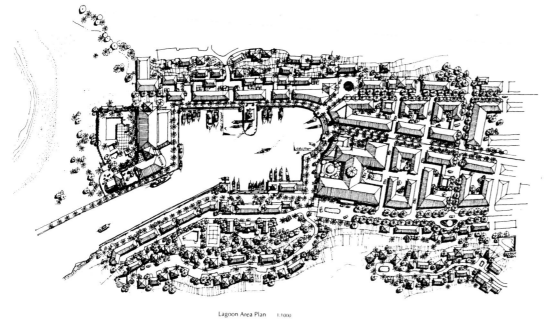

Lagoon Area Plan 1:1000

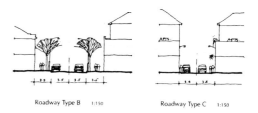

Roadway Type B 1:150

Roadway Type C 1:150

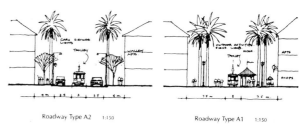

Roadway Type A2 1:150

Roadway Type A1 1:150

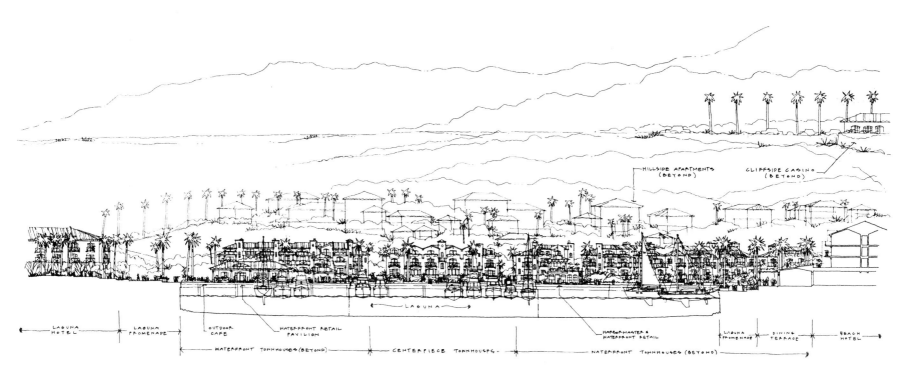

HILLSIDE APARTMENTS
(BEYOND)

CLIFFSIDE CASINO
(BEYOND)

LAGUNA

LAGUNA
HOTEL

LAGUNA
PROMENADE

OUTDOOR
CAFE

WATERFRONT RETAIL
PAVILION

HARBORMASTER &
WATERFRONT RETAIL

LAGUNA
PROMENADE

DINING
TERRACE

BEACH
HOTEL

WATERFRONT TOWNHOUSES (BEYOND)

CENTERPIECE TOWNHOUSES

WATERFRONT TOWNHOUSES (BEYOND)

Lagoon Section Looking South   1:200

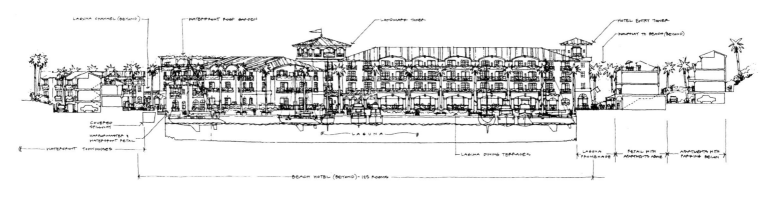

LAGUNA CHANNEL (BEYOND)

WATERFRONT ROOF GARDEN

LANDMARK TOWER

HOTEL ENTRY TOWER

WALKWAY TO BEACH (BEYOND)

COVERED SPILLWAY
HARBORMASTER & WATERFRONT RETAIL

WATERFRONT TOWNHOUSES

LAGUNA

LAGUNA DINING TERRACES

LAGUNA
PROMENADE

RETAIL WITH
APARTMENTS ABOVE

APARTMENTS WITH
PARKING BELOW

BEACH HOTEL (BEYOND) - 125 ROOMS

Lagoon Section Looking North   1:200

Line

Line Types

The basic graphic symbol for all plan and section drawings is line. Line defines spatial edges, renders volume, creates textures, and connects to form words and numbers. Linework in plan and section should be sharp and dense with uniform width and consistent value for the purpose of legibility. There are four basic line types: dotted, short-dashed, long-dashed, and continuous line; each type has a specific function and meaning.

Dotted or short-dashed lines represent unseen edges of an object. Continuous lines represent the visible edges. Short-dashed lines in general represent hidden or unseen objects in front of or below the observer. In plan drawings, these lines are often used to indicate objects underground. In sections and elevations, they are often used to indicate the location of objects behind any opaque planes.

Long-dashed lines in general represent hidden or unseen objects behind or above the observer. They also indicate items within the construction limit that are to be removed. For example, the roof overhang line in a floor plan is often represented with long-dashed lines. Existing contour lines are shown with long-dashed lines while finished or reshaped contours are drawn with continuous lines.

line

dotted line

short -dashed line

long-dashed line

continuous line

41

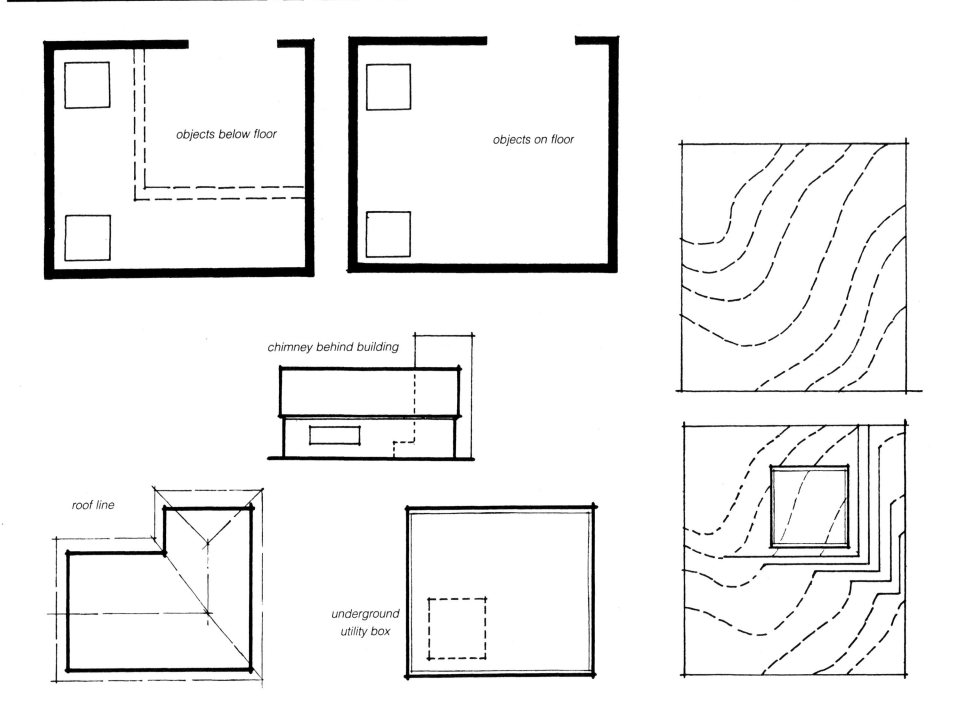

objects below floor

objects on floor

chimney behind building

roof line

underground utility box

———————— SAS ———————— sanitary sewer

———————— STS ———————— storm sewer

———————— COS ———————— combined sewer

— — — DRT — — — drain tile

— · — CLL — · — contract-limit line

— — · — PRL — — · — property line

———————— G ———————— gas main

———————— O ———————— fuel-oil main

———————— T ———————— telephone line

———————— W ———————— water main

———————— P ———————— power line

————— CL ————— centerline of road
(usually in dashes)

—×—×—×—×—×—×— fence

new building

existing building to remain

existing building to be removed

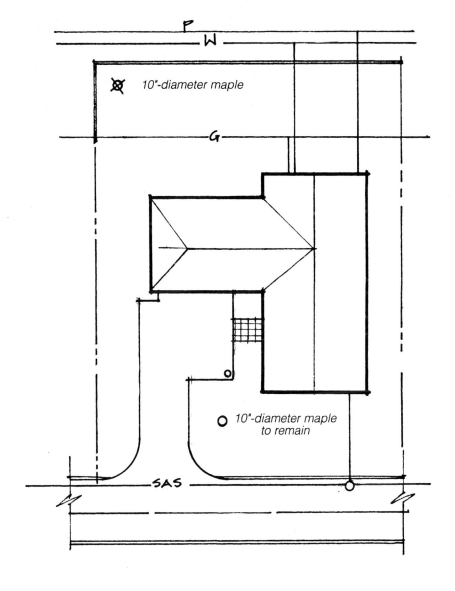

P

W

10"-diameter maple

G

10"-diameter maple
to remain

SAS

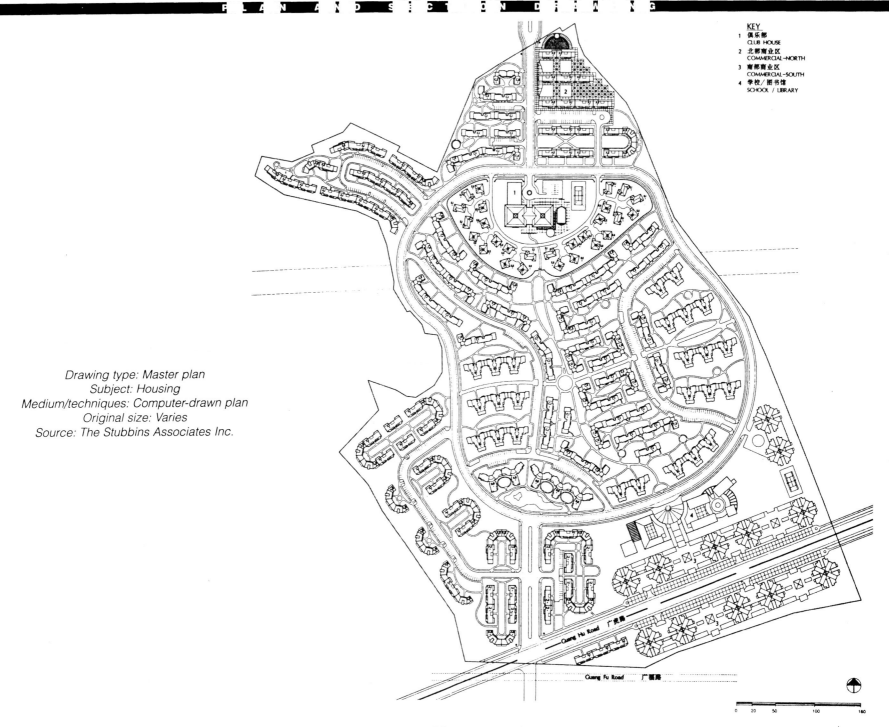

KEY

1 俱乐部
CLUB HOUSE

2 北郡商业区
COMMERCIAL-NORTH

3 南郡商业区
COMMERCIAL-SOUTH

4 学校／图书馆
SCHOOL / LIBRARY

Drawing type: Master plan
Subject: Housing
Medium/techniques: Computer-drawn plan
Original size: Varies
Source: The Stubbins Associates Inc.

Guang Fu Road 广福路

Guang Fu Road 广福路

0   20   50   100   150

Line Width

There are four basic line widths: extra thick, thick, medium, and thin. These are arbitrary subdivisions and there are no standardized measurements for each width. The width of lines is relative and depends largely on the content and the overall size of the drawings. Thin lines may be quite appropriate for a small drawing but become invisible in a large and busy plan. In principle, thick lines are used for objects closer to the observer and thin lines are used for objects farther from the observer. Strong spatial edges such as an edge of a building or the edge of a tree should be rendered with thicker lines than elements that do not have such a strong vertical break. Paving patterns fall into this category.

Double lines are used to accentuate major spatial edges such as the cornice of a building, walls, or curbs. In general, double lines of different widths are more legible and less confusing than similar line widths.

extra thick line

thick line

medium line

thin line

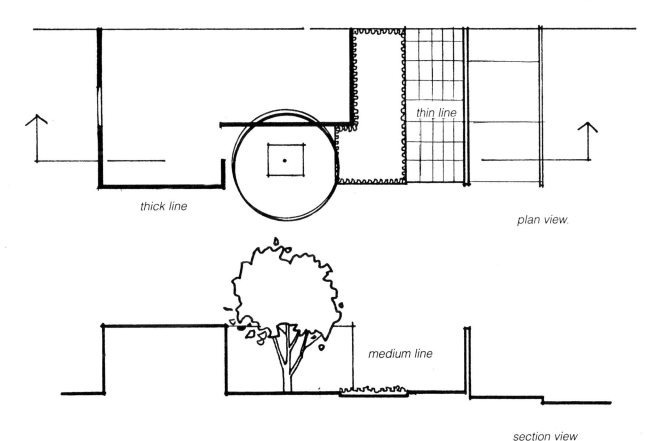

thin line

thick line

plan view.

medium line

section view

In a working drawing, profile lines of construction details should be drawn with a thick line. Use thin or extra thin lines for texturing the materials. Dimension lines should be thin with a heavy short dash at the dimension-line intersection.

construction detail

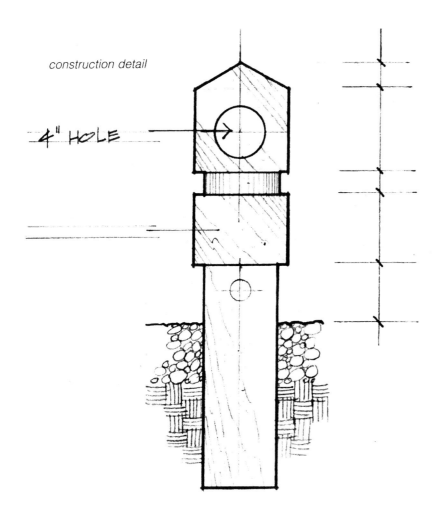

4" HOLE

In a section or elevation drawing, profile lines of the ground should be drawn with a relatively thick line. Edges of trees should be connected with a medium line. Objects at a distance should be outlined with a thin line.

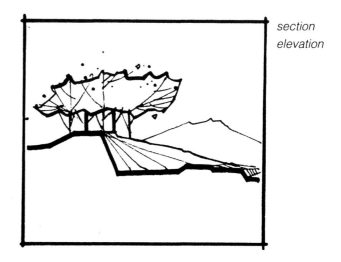

section elevation

In a plan view a building edge—or wall—should be drawn with a thick line. Design elements—benches and plantings—should be rendered with a medium line. Edges of trees should be gone over with a thick border. Use a thin line for patterns and textures.

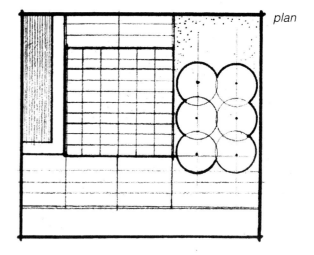

plan

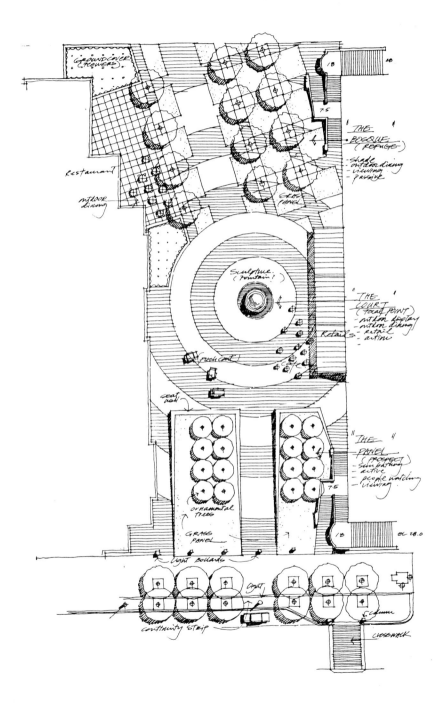

Quality of Line

The quality of line depends largely on the drawing medium. It is the designer's responsibility to represent the message clearly and without ambiguity. In architecture and engineering related matters, there are standard symbols and line types for a designer to use. Landscape drawing tends to be less restrictive but designers likewise have to follow many of these symbols, especially when relocation of utilities and moving earth are involved. As a matter of fact, plans and sections produced in design development and construction document phases must follow these trade standards without deviation. Since these drawings are often used for cost estimation, they must be drawn precisely to represent their intentions. CADD drawings are therefore indispensable, especially in the production of construction documents.

The quality of line can be more fluid and expressive in the schematic and conceptual design phases. These drawings focus primarily on the design message and are therefore less restricted by standards and formats. Depending on the design subject, conceptual and schematic plan and section drawings are more likely to emphasize the artistic side of the message. Line quality in these drawings becomes more poetic and lively than their counterparts in design development and construction documents both of which can be static and lifeless. The contrast in line quality is relative, not absolute. Design process governs the diversity. Subject matter sometimes dictates the difference. A situation such as presentation may decide the choices. Ultimately it is the designer who should make the choice based on his or her skills and talents. This is called one's best professional judgment.

Drawing type: Schematic plan
Subject: Urban park
Medium/techniques: Pilot razorpoint on white tracing paper
Original size: 18" x 24"
Source: Wang Associates International

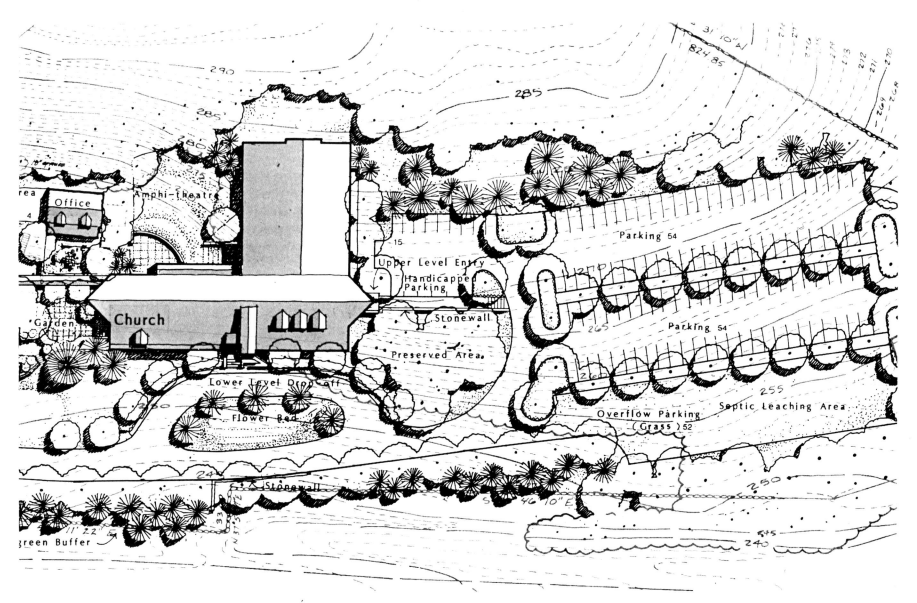

Office

Amphi-theatre

rea

4

Garden

Church

Lower Level Drop-off

Flower Bed

green Buffer

250

6' X Stonewall

11' 22

33

290

285

285

280

275

15

Upper Level Entry

Handicapped Parking

Stonewall

Preserved Area

270

265

260

255

Parking 54

Parking 54

Overflow Parking (Grass) 52

Septic Leaching Area

250

S 46 10" E

245

240

31 10" W

824.85

270

273

272

271

270

269

268

Drawing type: Site plan
Subject: Institutional planning
Medium/techniques: Ink pen on photographic mylar (topographic base screened)
Original size: 30" x 42"
Source: Wang Associates International

Plan Graphics

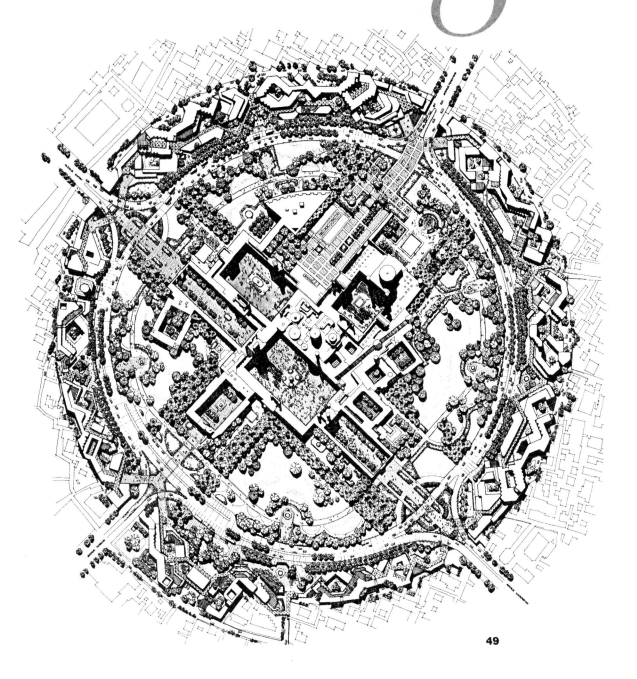

Architecture

The plan looks at buildings from the top. It emphasizes the horizontal dimension of the structure and the way it relates to the surroundings. Edges of buildings should be bold, crisp, and accurately drawn. Roof line, including the pitches and details on the roof, can give a plain, flat roof a more sculptural look. Shadow brings out the three-dimensional quality of the buildings. It can depict the height of the buildings, differentiate season and the time of day, and indicate the surface condition of the surrounding ground.

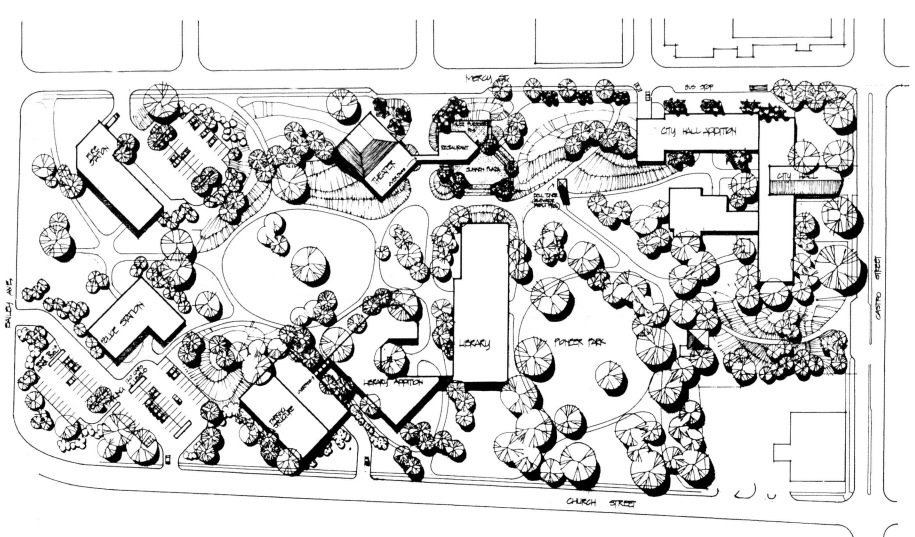

MOUNTAIN VIEW CIVIC CENTER
MOUNTAIN VIEW, CALIFORNIA

NORTH
SCALE: 1"= 40'-0'

A thin line drawing has weak spatial edges. They should be differentiated from the rest of the lines representing other design elements.

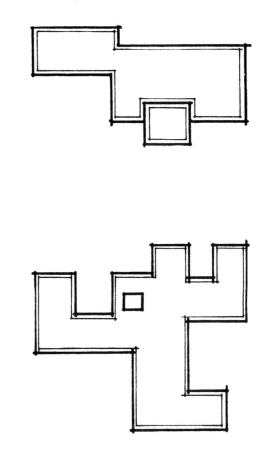

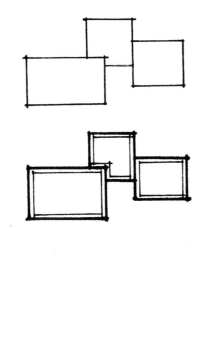

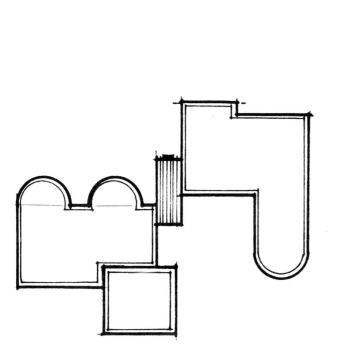

A thick profile line with a thin line inside. This double line begins to define a stronger edge and gives the building a more massive appearance.

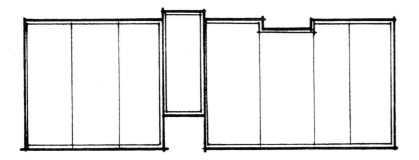

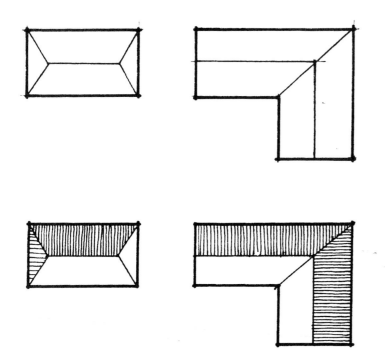

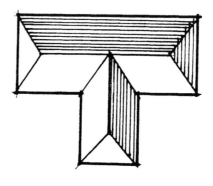

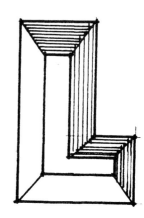

A building with a pitch roof should be textured to increase the three-dimensional quality. Roofs without texture tend to have flat appearances.

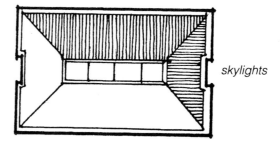

skylights

In texturing a roof, begin to bring out the feeling of depth. This gives the viewer a better understanding of the roof form.

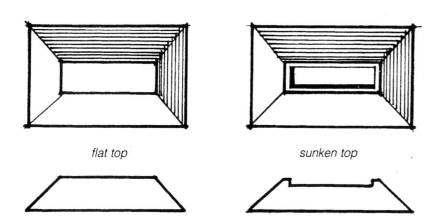

flat top   *sunken top*

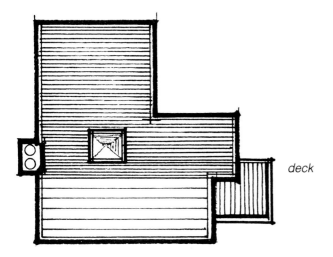

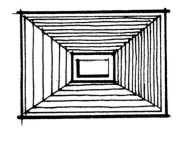

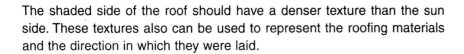

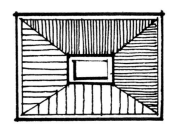

deck

enclosed court

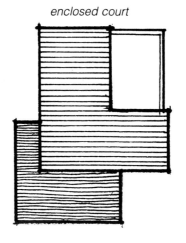

The shaded side of the roof should have a denser texture than the sun side. These textures also can be used to represent the roofing materials and the direction in which they were laid.

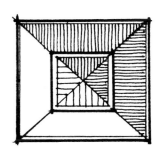

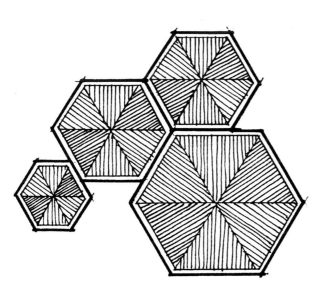

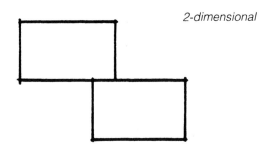

2-dimensional

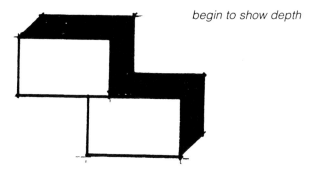

begin to show depth

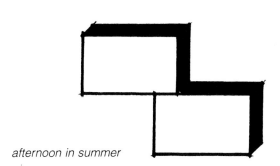

afternoon in summer

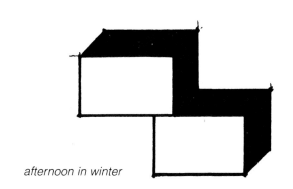

afternoon in winter

building B is taller than building A

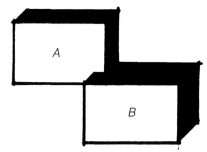

buildings A and B are the same height

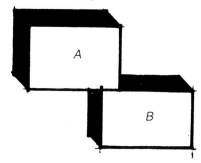

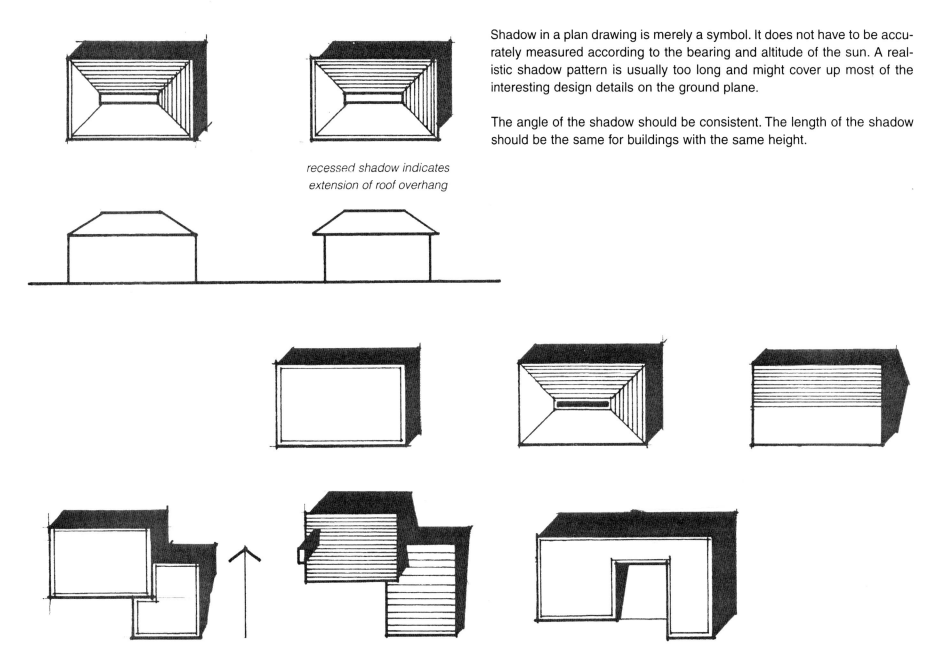

Shadow in a plan drawing is merely a symbol. It does not have to be accurately measured according to the bearing and altitude of the sun. A realistic shadow pattern is usually too long and might cover up most of the interesting design details on the ground plane.

The angle of the shadow should be consistent. The length of the shadow should be the same for buildings with the same height.

recessed shadow indicates
extension of roof overhang

ground slopes   *roof slopes*   *ramp*

A more realistic shadow for the Northern Hemisphere.

shadow up

Some artists think that the shadow reads better when it is pointing down.

shadow down

For a short shadow, this design provides maximum contrast and opacity.

solid black

This style has a nice semitransparent texture but takes time to draw.

cross-hatching

This has good texture but is easily confused with other lines on the ground plane, especially pavements.

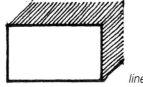

line

This saves time and is easy to use but is incompatible with a hand-drawn plan.

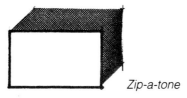

Zip-a-tone

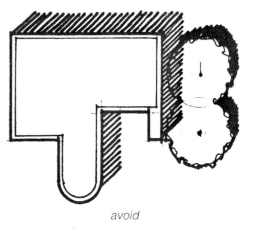

avoid

OK

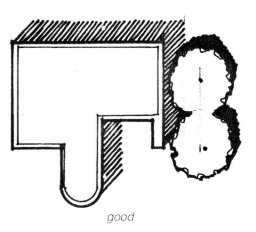

good

Drawing type: Site plan
Subject: Housing
Medium/techniques: Colored markers on blackline print
Original size: 36" x 24"
Source: Student work, University of Michigan

Vegetation

Vegetation is the most important symbol in landscape architecture plan drawing. Like buildings, plants create spaces, define spatial edges, provide shade, and add color to the environment. Properly drawn plant materials enhance the plan drawing.

Vegetation is divided into three subcategories: trees, shrubs, and ground covers. Trees and ground covers are usually drawn with a circular outline to indicate the spread of the canopy. This simple geometric representation provides a more organic counterpart to the rectangularly drawn architectural subjects. These circles should be outlined with thin pencils first, with a circle template, to ensure that they are uniform and consistent. The outlines are then traced over in freehand with a thicker line. Double lines are often used to delineate the forest edge.

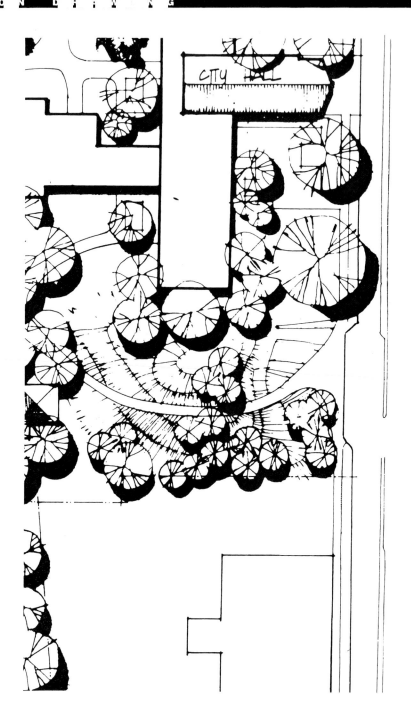

Trees

The canopy of the matured trees extends and overlaps one another in nature. Tree symbols look better when they are slightly overlapped in a plan drawing. Of course, spacing trees is a design decision and other spacing orders must be observed as well. Overlapping symbols should be carefully planned so that they do not interfere or block the other symbols underneath them.

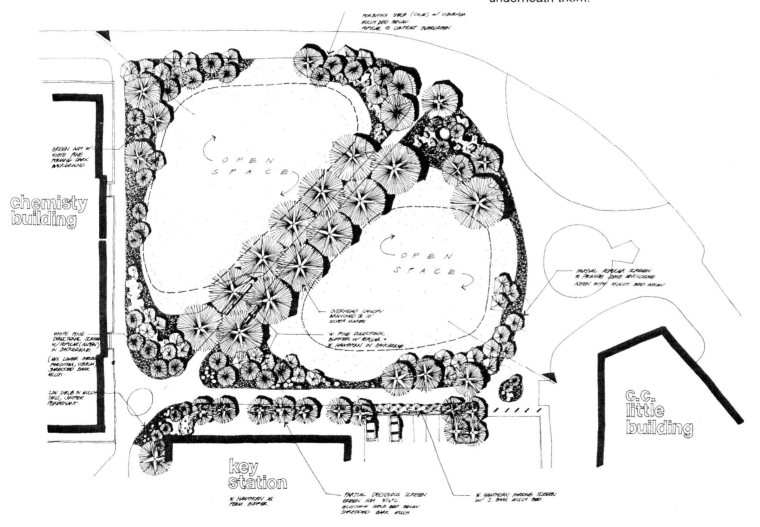

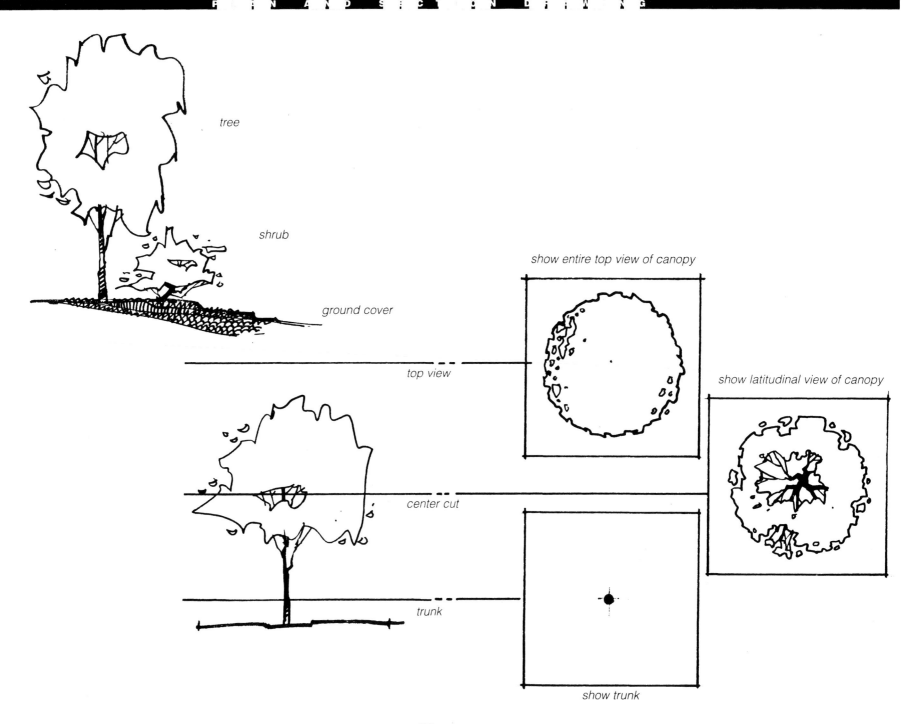

tree

shrub

ground cover

top view

center cut

trunk

show entire top view of canopy

show latitudinal view of canopy

show trunk

There are three basic ways to draw trees in plan: branch, outline, and texture. Outline has a solid, opaque appearance. Plant materials and other design elements are usually not shown underneath this kind of symbol. Branch and texture are more realistic. The silhouette effect of these styles allows the viewer to see through the canopy. However, including the objects underneath the canopy can undermine the simplicity and clarity of the symbol.

actual

branch

outline

texture

deciduous trees

evergreen trees

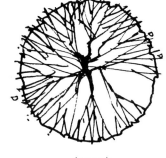

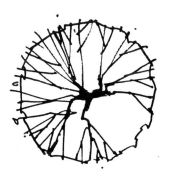

examples of tree symbols

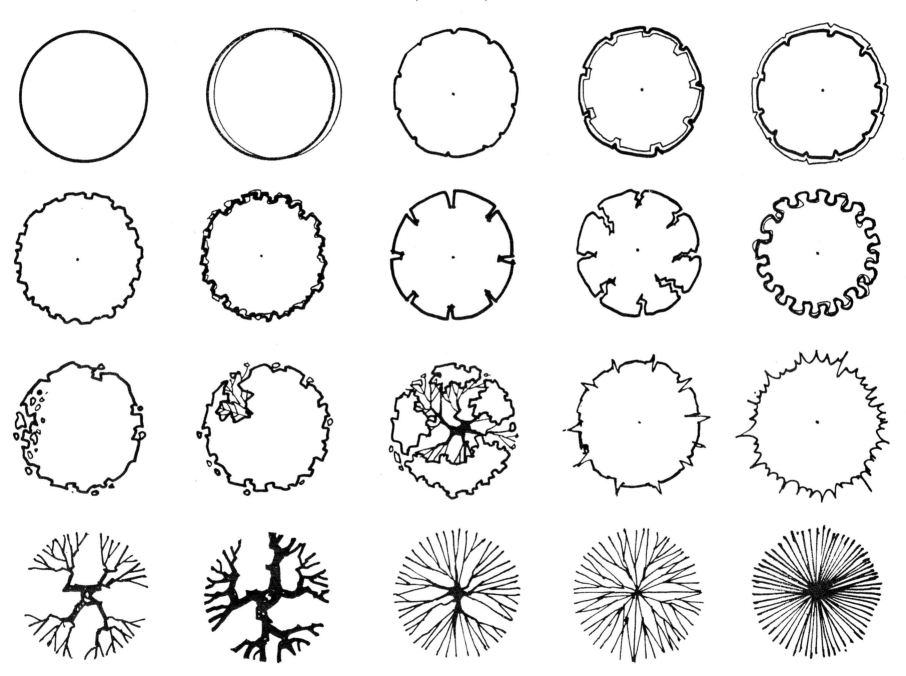

The major function of plant material is to make space. Trees are often shown in groups to create a more defined edge.

Overlapping should be carefully avoided. Outline the tree edge with a thick line. Use a thin pencil line to define individual trees.

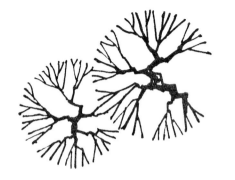

Avoid overlapping branch and texture symbols. Larger trees are always shown above smaller ones. Branches and textures should be carefully spaced to prevent excessive complexity when symbols overlap.

how to draw a tree in plan view

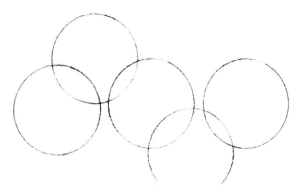

Draw a circle with the aid of a circle template.

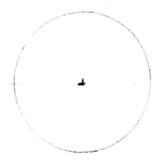

Plot the tree with a thin pencil outline. Use a circle template.

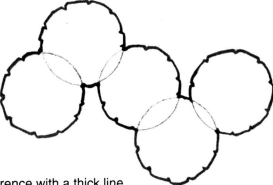

Outline the major branches with a soft pencil.

Select the appropriate symbol. Outline the circumference with a thick line.

Fill in the complete branching pattern. Do not go over the edge of the circle.

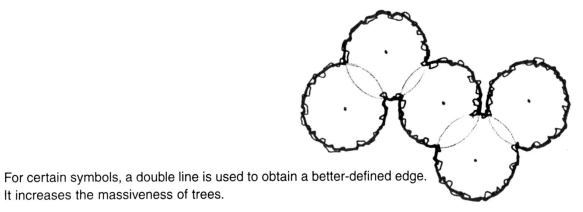

For certain symbols, a double line is used to obtain a better-defined edge. It increases the massiveness of trees.

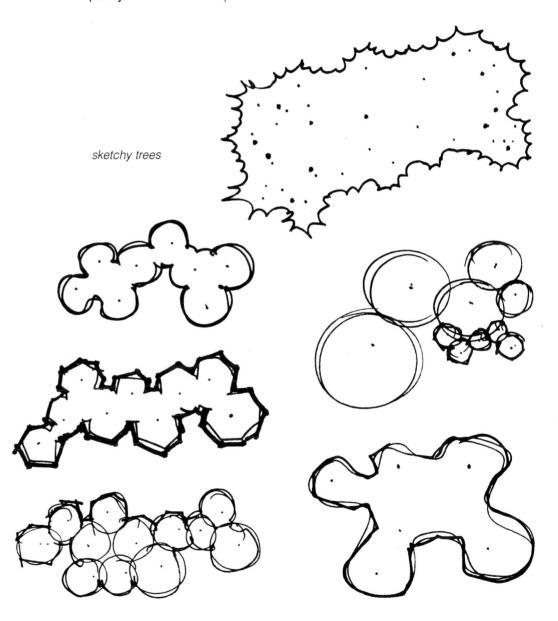

In most preliminary-design plans plantings are drawn freehand. Despite their sketchy appearance, these symbols should be drawn accurately and quickly.

sketchy trees

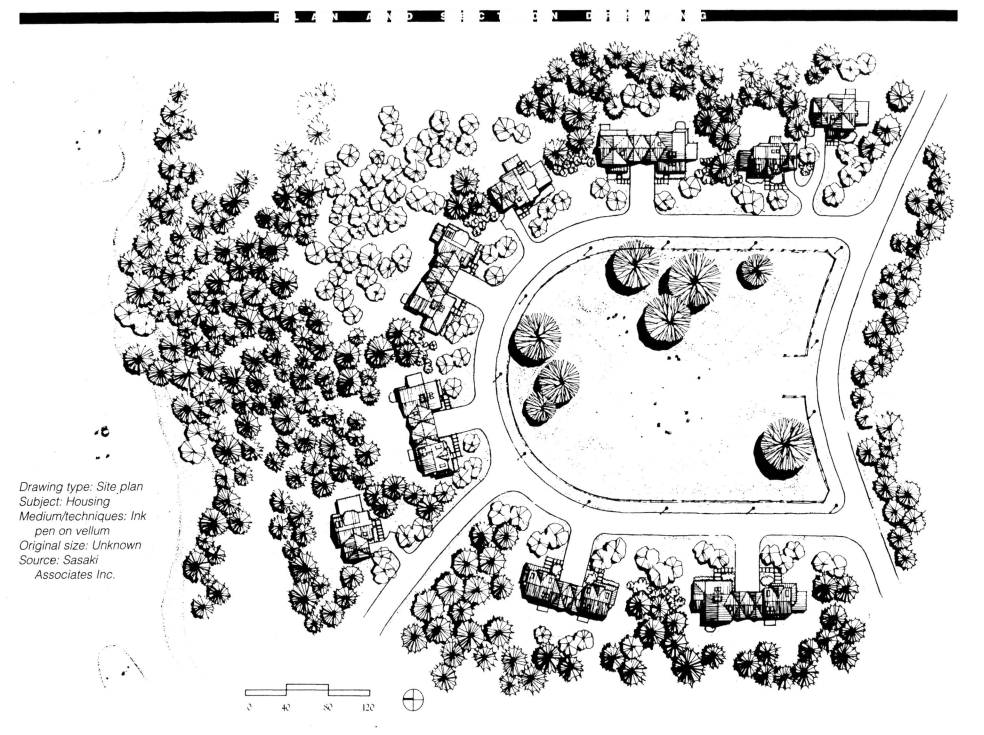

Drawing type: Site plan
Subject: Housing
Medium/techniques: Ink
   pen on vellum
Original size: Unknown
Source: Sasaki
   Associates Inc.

0   40   80   120

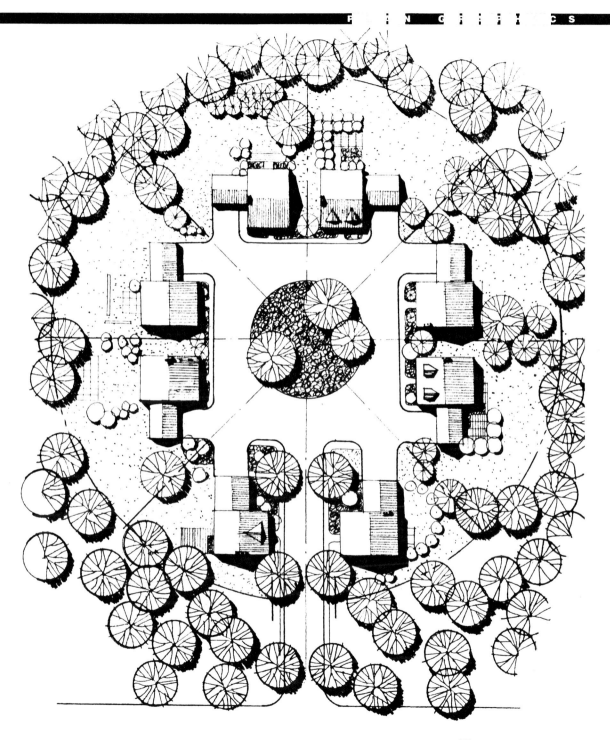

Shrubs

In plan drawings shrub symbols are the same as trees except that they are often shown in groups. Depending on the scale and content of the drawing, outline symbols are usually more simple and appropriate than the branch and texture types. Branch and texture shrub symbols are especially inappropriate when used with trees rendered in similar fashion.

plan view

elevation

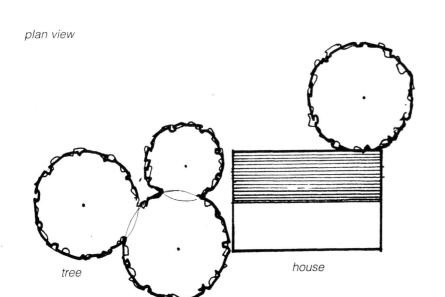

tree

house

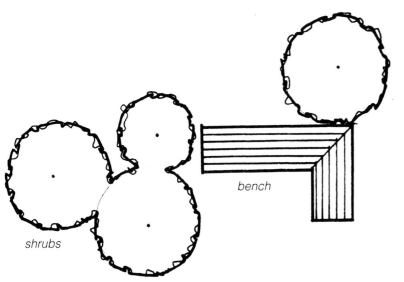

shrubs

bench

shrubs are usually planted in groups

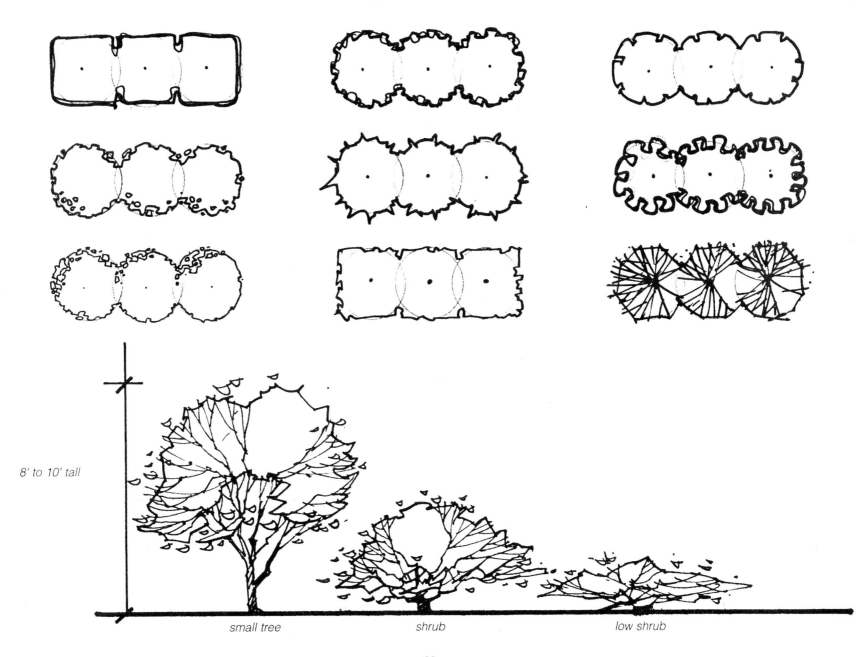

8' to 10' tall

small tree   shrub   low shrub

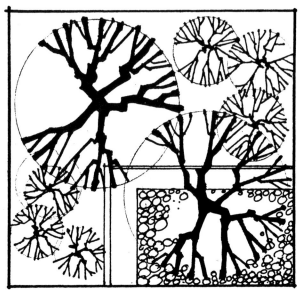

bad

Outline symbols are more appropriate for small shrubs because of their massive and solid look. Texture and branch symbols are too busy and complex for the smaller shrubs. They are especially inappropriate when shrubs are used with trees.

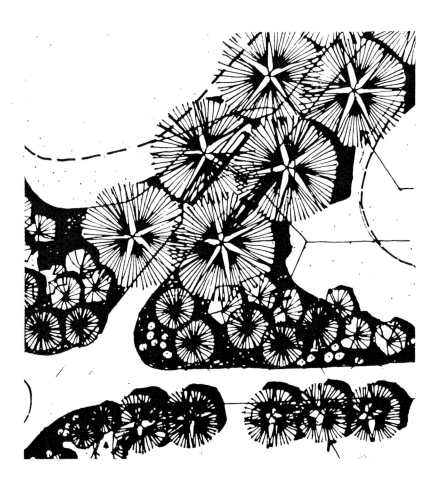

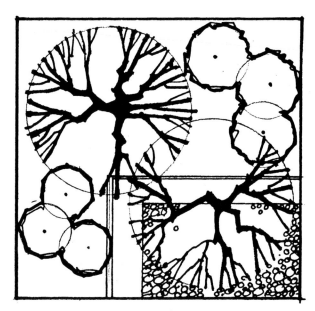

good

70

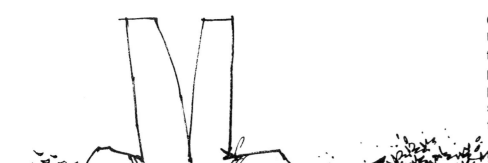

Ground Covers

Ground covers include low, creeping plant materials as well as grass. Unlike trees and shrubs, which are portrayed graphically as objects above the ground, ground covers in general form a continuous background in plan drawing. A drawing without background materials tends to overemphasize the objects on top—trees and buildings—resulting in a busy and spotty drawing. Background materials de-emphasize the individuality of these parts and brings them together harmoniously.

texture is the combination of lines

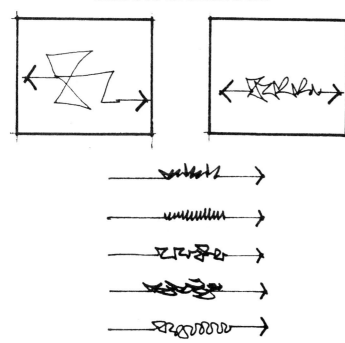

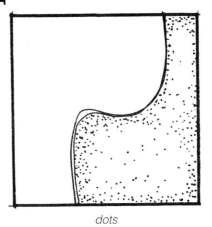

dots

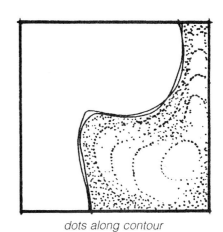

dots along contour

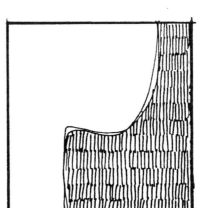

line

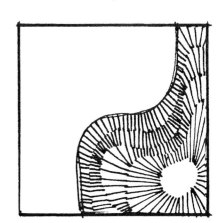

line along contour

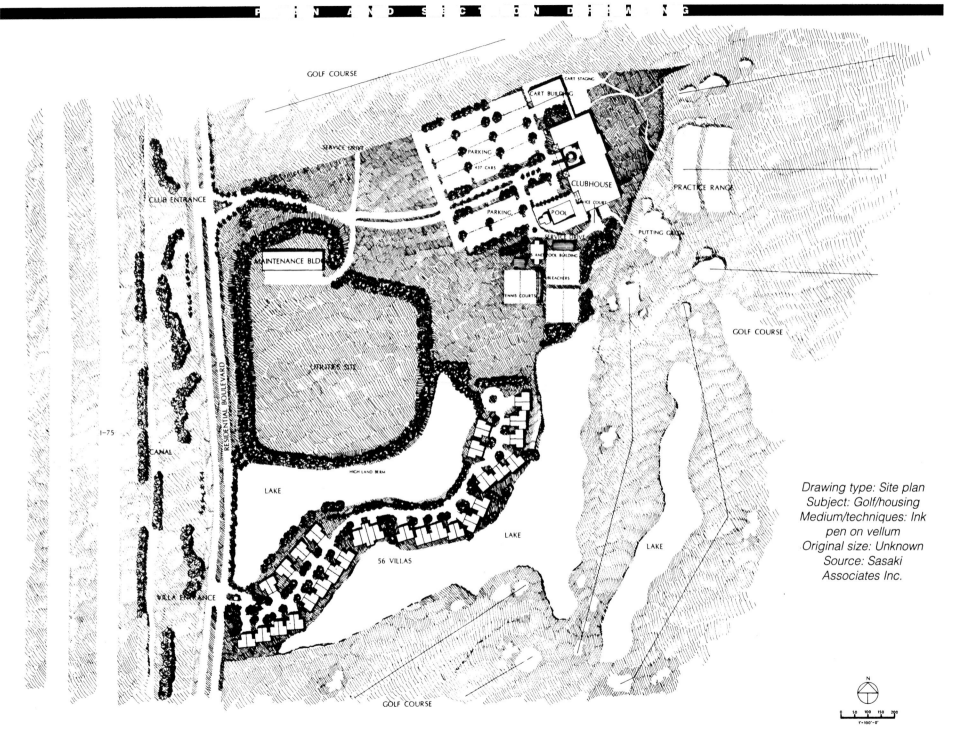

GOLF COURSE

CART STAGING

CART BUILDING

PARKING
437 CARS

CLUBHOUSE

PRACTICE RANGE

SERVICE DRIVE

PARKING

POOL

SERVICE COURT

CLUB ENTRANCE

PUTTING GREEN

SERVICE DRIVE

MAINTENANCE BLDG

AND POOL BUILDING

BLEACHERS

TENNIS COURTS

GOLF COURSE

UTILITIES SITE

I-75

CANAL

RESIDENTIAL BOULEVARD

HIGH LAND BERM

LAKE

LAKE

LAKE

56 VILLAS

VILLA ENTRANCE

GOLF COURSE

Drawing type: Site plan
Subject: Golf/housing
Medium/techniques: Ink
pen on vellum
Original size: Unknown
Source: Sasaki
Associates Inc.

N

0 50 100 150 200
1"=100'-0"

Textures of ground covers should be carefully selected to blend with other symbols. Their intensity should be even and their line width should be consistent. Avoid varying textures in the same drawing. Excessive differentiation tends to increase the complexity of the plan image and to confuse the viewers.

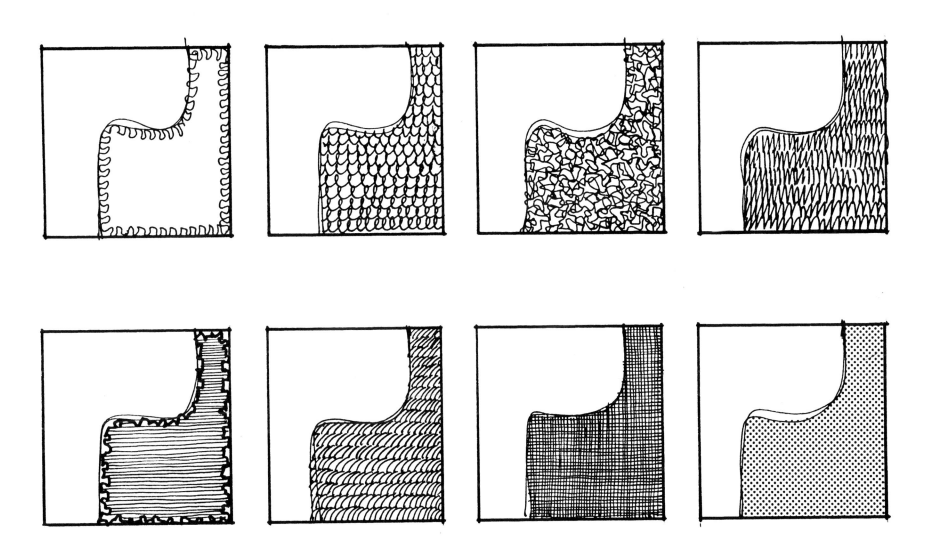

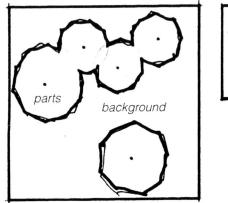

parts

background

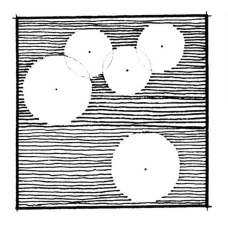

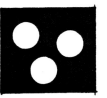

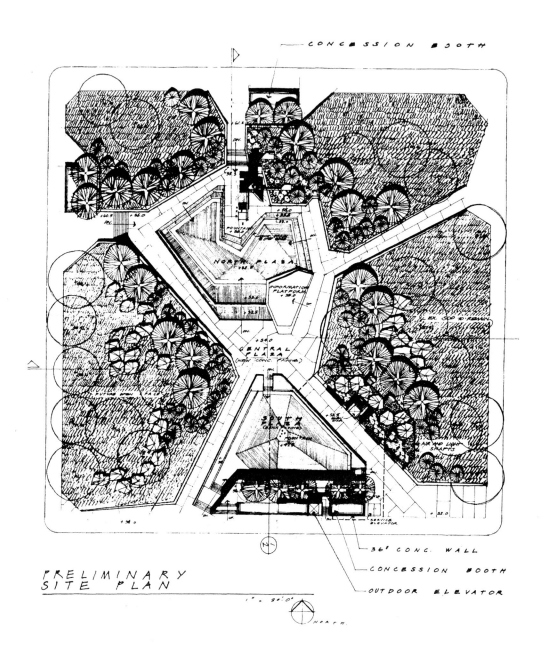

PRELIMINARY
SITE PLAN

elevation

level 1

level 2

level 3

level 4

Overlappings and Shadows

Overlapping branch symbols should be carefully spaced so that they do not interfere or block the other symbols underneath them. It is very important for the viewers to complete the edges of these symbols visually. Overlapped edges should be drawn with a thinner line to minimize their complexity.

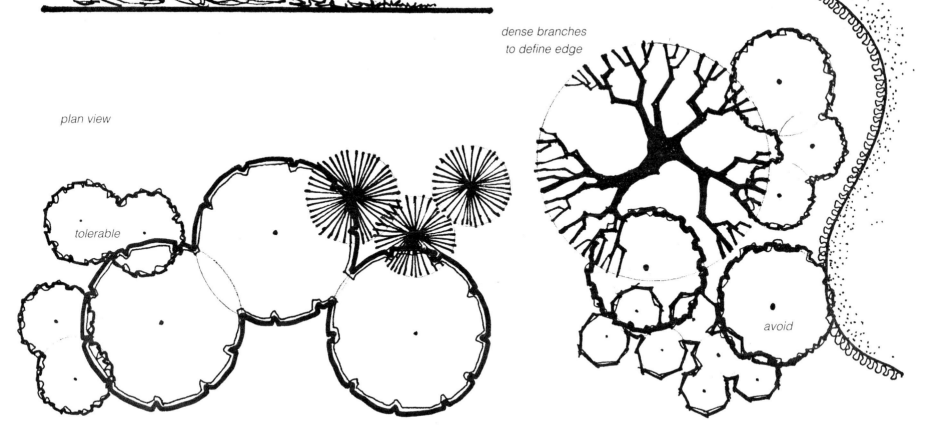

plan view

tolerable

dense branches to define edge

avoid

Avoid shadows shaped like an oil drum. The top of a tree is not flat.

The canopy of a tree is usually rounded with the center as its high point. The shadow of the tree should be longer in the center and gradually slope toward the edges.

Evergreens have a conical profile. The shadow of an evergreen is long and pointed. It has a triangular shape.

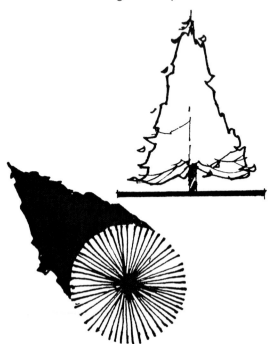

direction of strokes

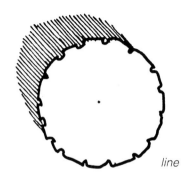

line

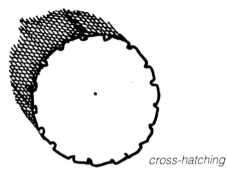

cross-hatching

thick marker line

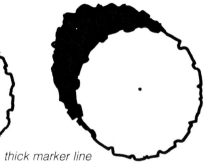

extra thick marker line

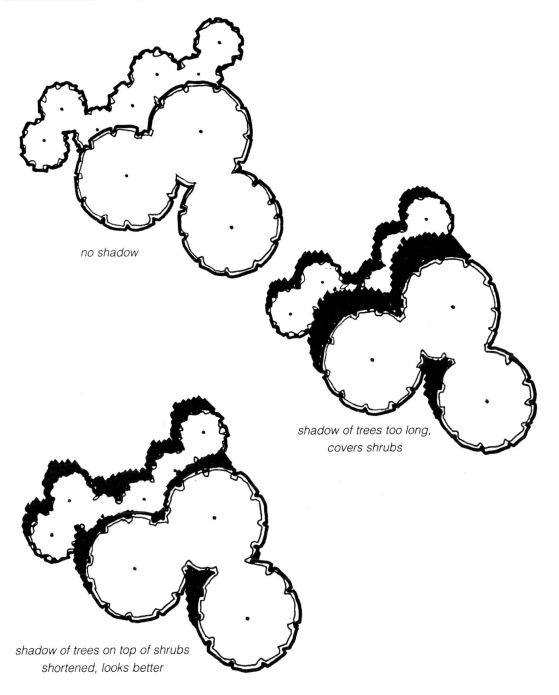

no shadow

shadow of trees too long, covers shrubs

shadow of trees on top of shrubs shortened, looks better

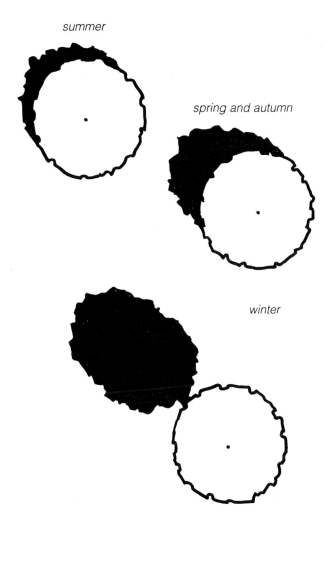

shadows and time

summer

spring and autumn

winter

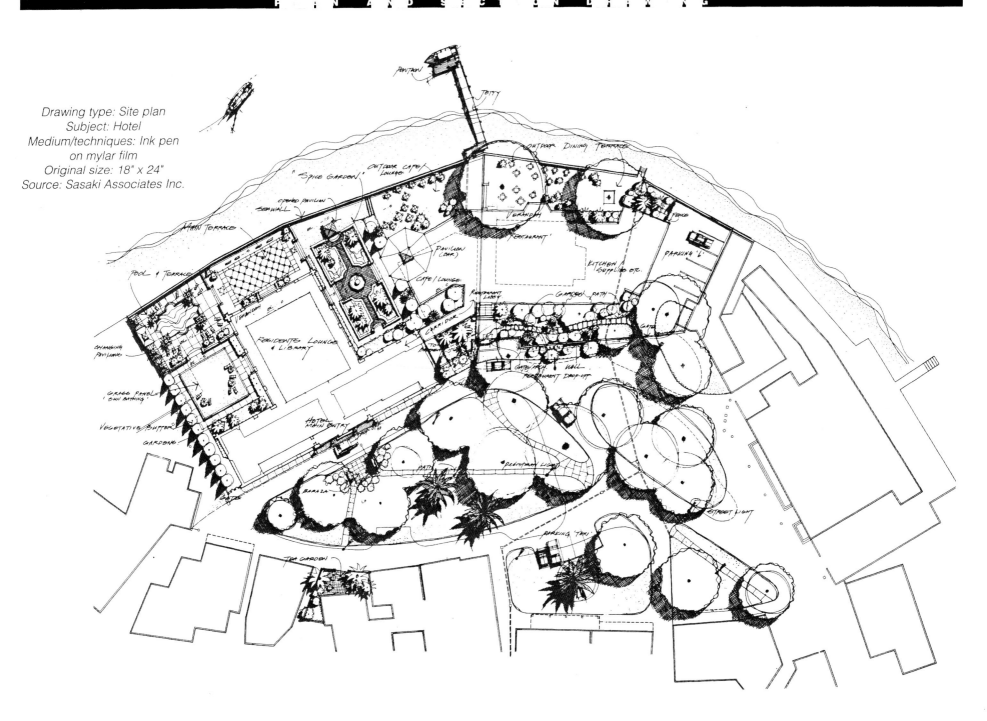

Drawing type: Site plan
Subject: Hotel
Medium/techniques: Ink pen
on mylar film
Original size: 18" x 24"
Source: Sasaki Associates Inc.

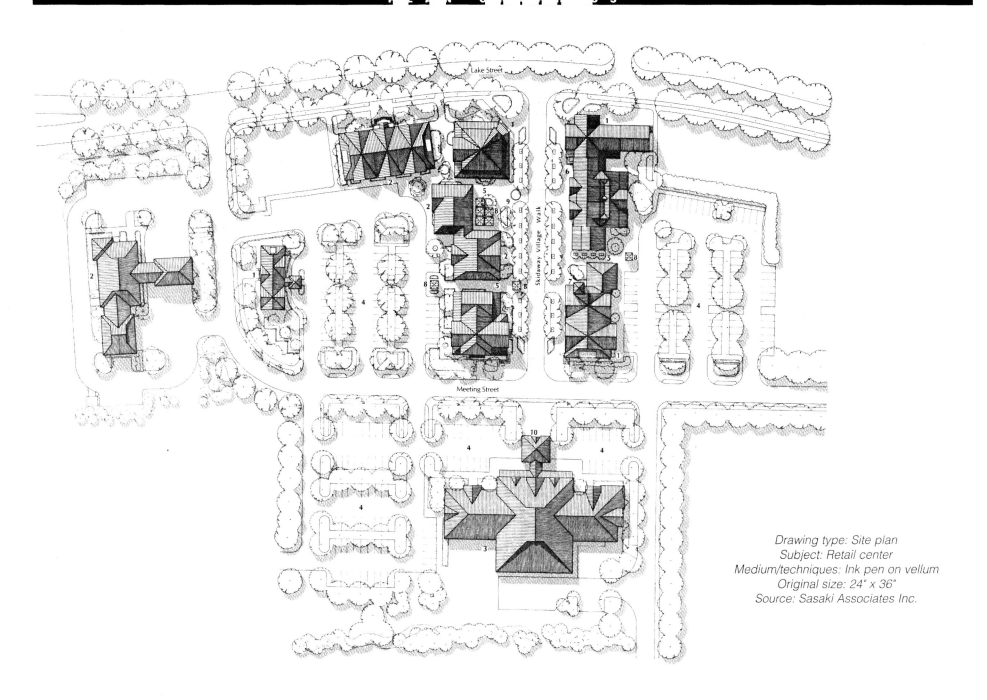

Lake Street

Skidaway Village Walk

Meeting Street

Drawing type: Site plan
Subject: Retail center
Medium/techniques: Ink pen on vellum
Original size: 24" x 36"
Source: Sasaki Associates Inc.

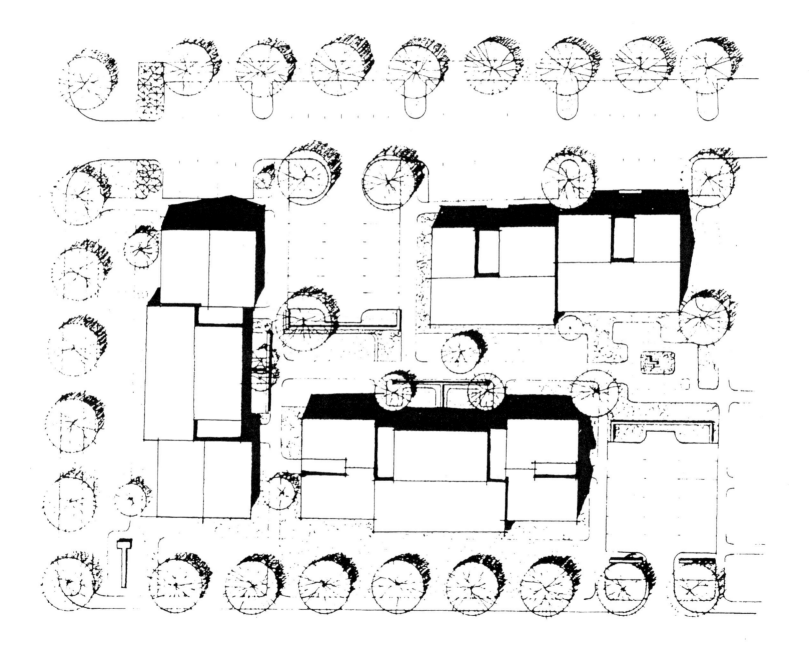

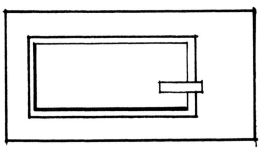

swimming pool

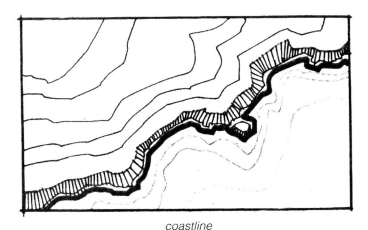

coastline

Water

Water features in plan drawing can be both a curse and a blessing. Water can animate a dull drawing by adding color and sparkles. However, a poor choice of color or texture can quickly ruin a drawing. Unlike grass which can also cover a relatively large area in a plan, water is unique because it has no other plan vocabulary that it can relate to. Grass relates to shrubs and trees and they share similarity in textures and color schemes. Grass can also relate easily to buildings and other paved surfaces. On the other hand, water cannot be easily rendered in texture because it tends to be read as an entirely different set of textural patterns and can cause visual distraction. For example, a ripple effect in the waves may be a logical and appropriate way to represent water, but its circular and repetitious texture can upset the visual balance of a plan.

A simple way to show water is by identifying its edge. The edge (shoreline or the edge or pool) defines the limit of the water body and also gives the viewer a hint of its function and characteristics. Edges also reinforce the contrast between the water and the land. The best way to highlight water is to create a uniform tonal background by either masking or airbrush. The tonal contrast makes the water recede without competing with the design of the land.

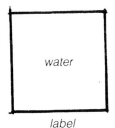

label

Zip-a-tone

show fathom line

show ripple

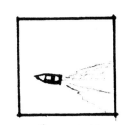

show waves

The water in this example is rendered dark to bring out the contrast between it and the land.

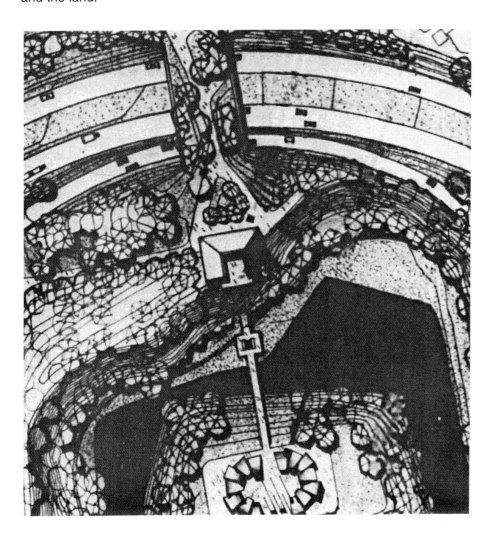

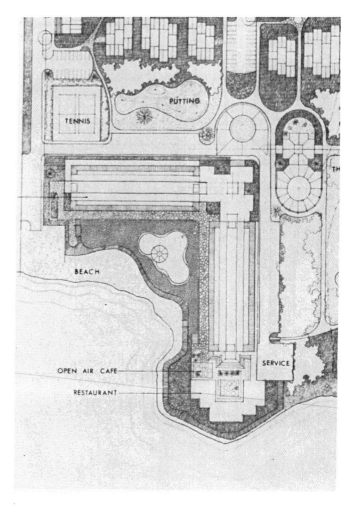

The water in this example is rendered by a few lines drawn parallel to the shoreline. These lines indicate the gradual change in the water depth.

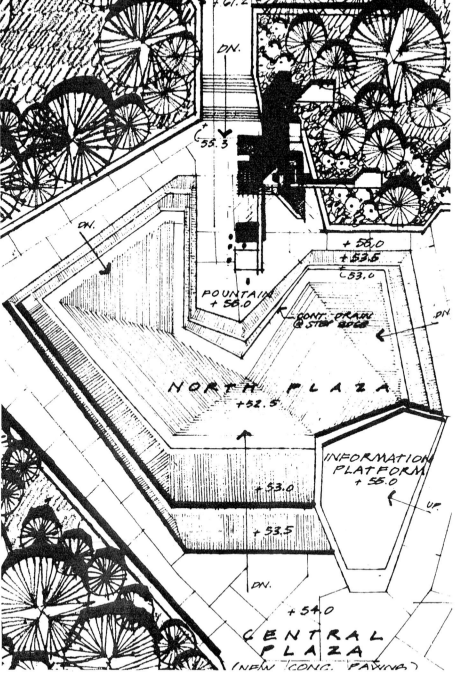

Pavement

Pavement, like ground covers, is also a kind of background material in plan drawing. It also has the ability to bring parts together. Pavement includes plaza, roadway, sidewalk, steps, decking, patio, and any walking surfaces. Pavement symbols vary from project to project. Most of these symbols are simplified expressions of the real thing. They graphically represent the surface condition as well as the pattern of the materials. The amount of detail and texture depends on the scale and size of the drawing. For example, showing individual brick paving on a 1" = 200.00' scale plan is not only inappropriate but a waste of time. Assess the overall visual quality and use your common sense in selecting these symbols.

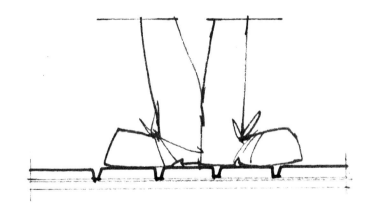

outline

texture

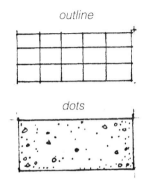

dots

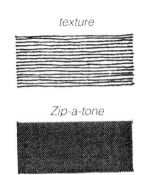

Zip-a-tone

typical pavement symbols

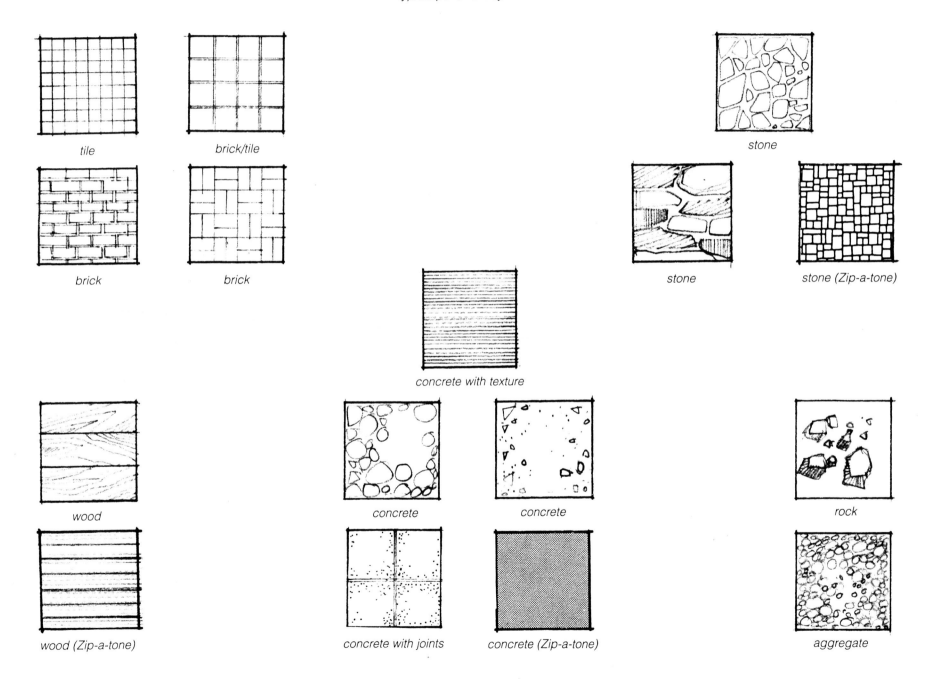

tile

brick/tile

stone

brick

brick

stone

stone (Zip-a-tone)

concrete with texture

wood

concrete

concrete

rock

wood (Zip-a-tone)

concrete with joints

concrete (Zip-a-tone)

aggregate

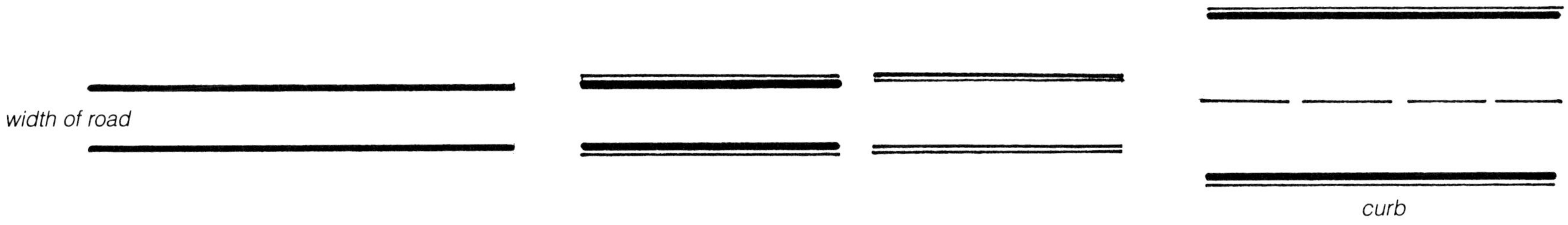

width of road

curb

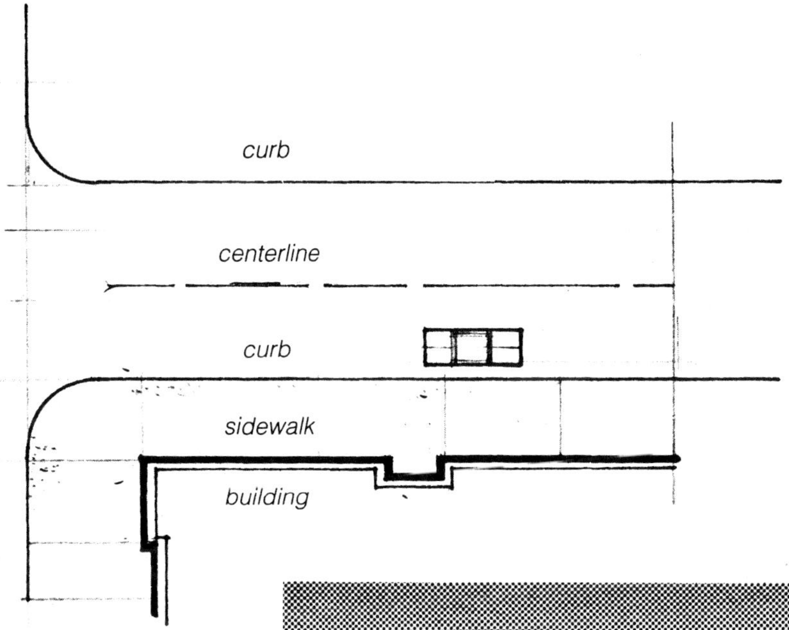

curb

centerline

A single line does not have a strong spatial edge. Double lines are more defined and are often used to indicate curb cuts.

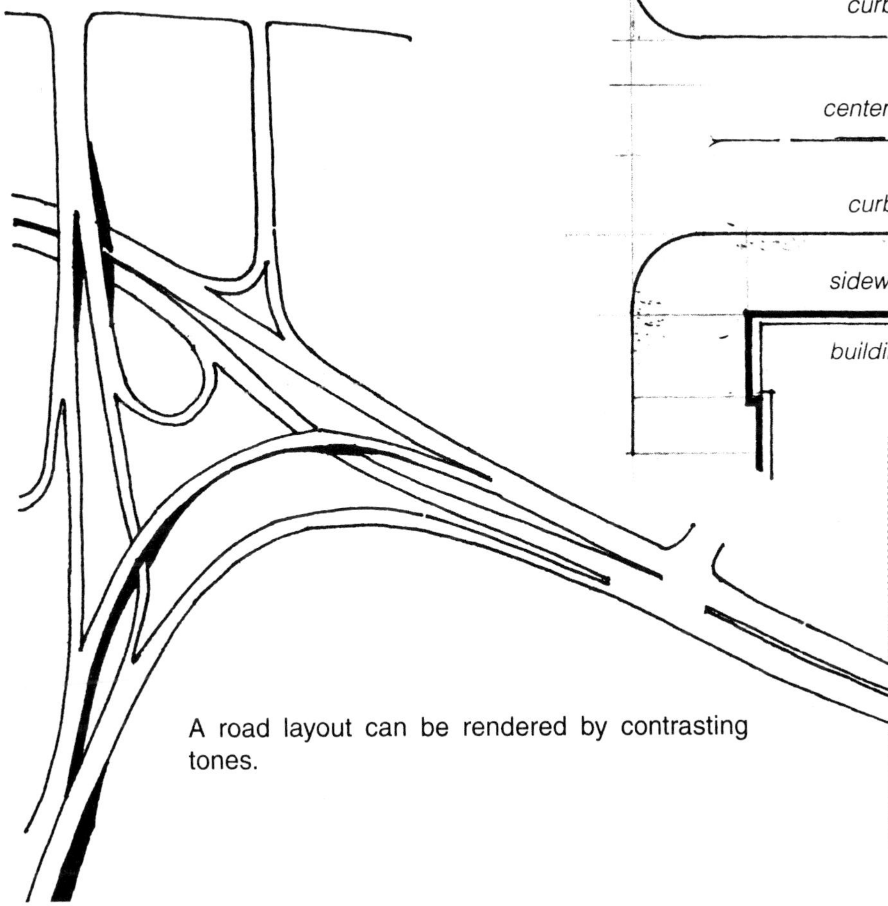

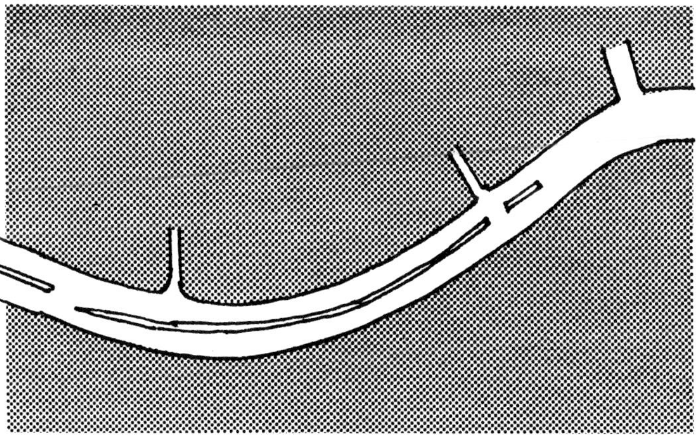

curb

sidewalk

building

A road layout can be rendered by contrasting tones.

Zip-a-tone

85

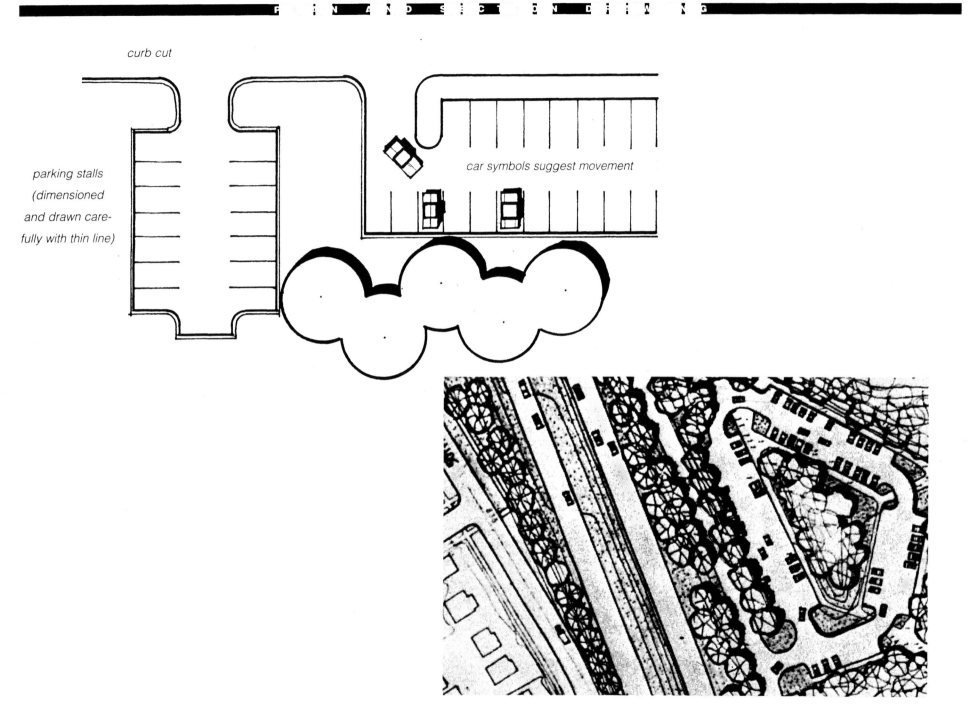

curb cut

parking stalls
(dimensioned
and drawn care-
fully with thin line)

car symbols suggest movement

use shadow to indicate change in elevation

road going through building

tunnel (underpass)

bridge (overpass)

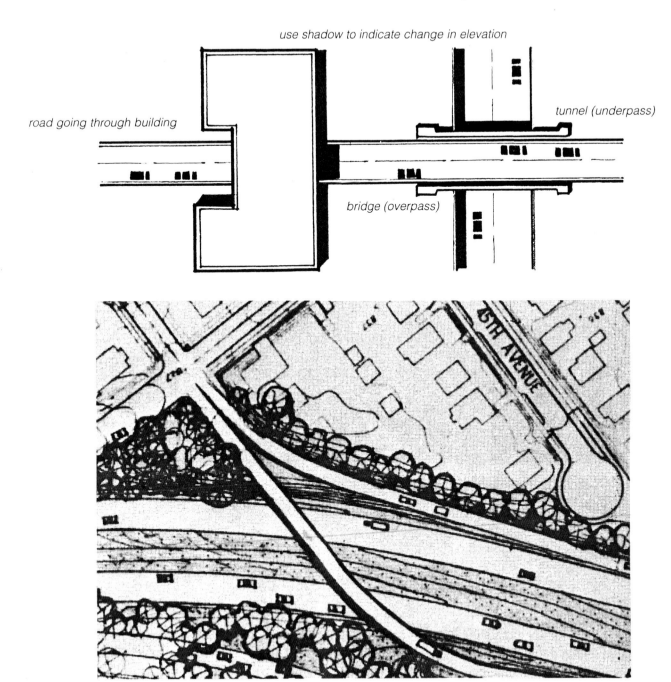

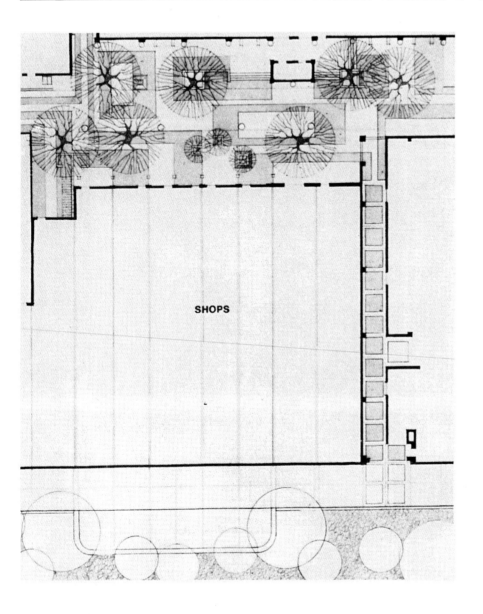

SHOPS

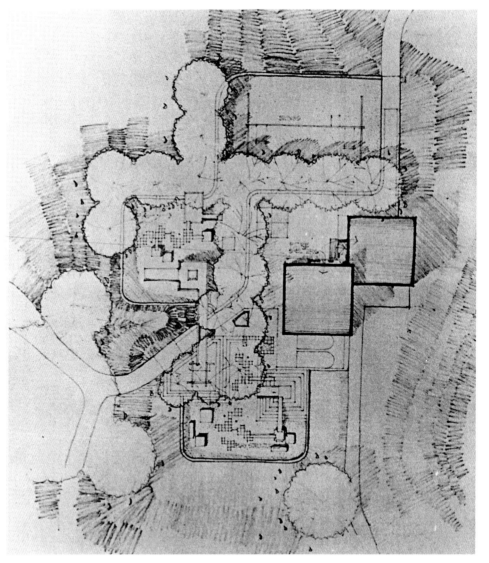

Others

In addition to architecture, vegetation, water, and ground, there are many other specifically designed features that appear on plan drawings. They include people, cars, benches, trellis, pushcarts, flagpoles, kiosks, boats, sculptures, lights, signs, and many others. Since each of the designs is unique and therefore differs from one another, there are no standards or uniform graphic symbols for each of the special features mentioned. A few suggestions are given in this book as references, but the best way is for each designer to create and invent his or her symbols that look good and can blend well within the entire picture context.

Cars, like boats and people, are decorative elements in plan drawing. They play supporting roles and enhance the quality of plan drawing. They are scale indicators as well as cues to the function of the design.

a car

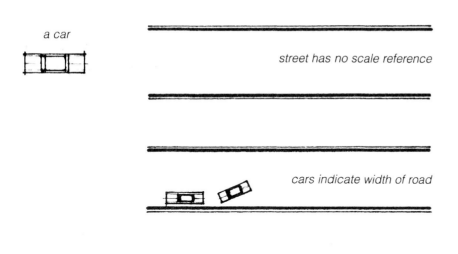

street has no scale reference

cars indicate width of road

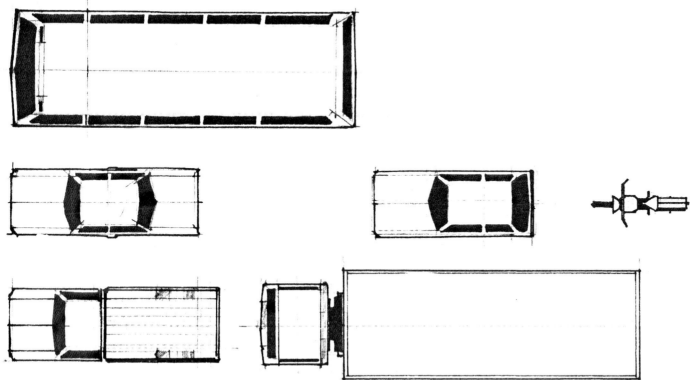

simple, symbolic

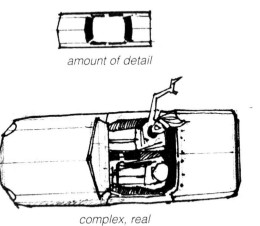

amount of detail

complex, real

Cars are not part of the design. They should not be overdone because excessive details will draw attention away from the design. They should be drawn to scale, however, and placed in accordance with traffic regulations.

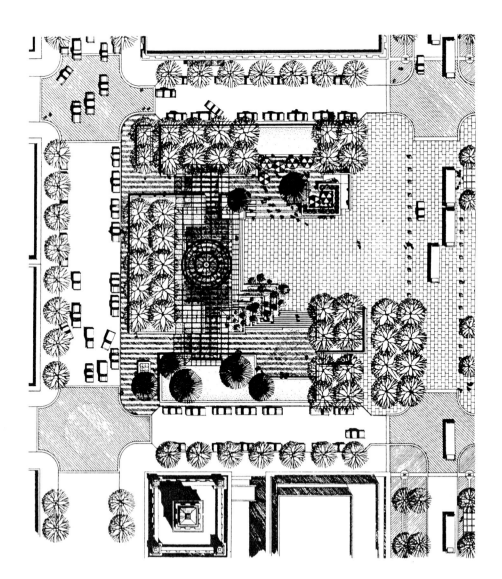

Sections and Elevations

Section and elevation drawings are more realistic and easier to understand than plan drawings. Unlike plan drawings which show only the view from above, section drawings show the view from the side as if the object is in front. This viewing position is more similar to the way we experience space visually and therefore presents a more realistic picture. Section drawings not only show the horizontal dimension but also the vertical dimension. With the cue of height the viewer can relate to the space and design more easily than with the two-dimensional plan.

Plan drawing is insufficient to communicate a design idea. Since it only deals with the horizontal dimension, a plan drawing must work with drawings that can show the vertical dimension so that a complete representation can be made. Section and elevation drawings are drawings that can do that.

Section drawing represents the conditions along the cut line. Cut line is an arbitrary line drawn across the plan with the intention to understand or reveal the vertical and horizontal conditions along it. In general, the cut line is often drawn across an area with many vertical grade changes or an area where architecture meets the land. Section drawing in this incident can reveal the need to install steps, a retaining wall, or a deck overlooking a magnificent view. In short, section drawings are strategic drawings used to compliment the plan and to provide the viewer with more information about the design. The number of section drawings required in a typical design is two: longitudinal and latitudinal. However, depending on the design problem and the complexity of the site, the designer can show as many of these drawings as necessary to present the design thoroughly. The key word is thorough and not redundant.

Technically speaking, section and elevation drawings are orthographic projections. In section drawing, the viewer is assumed to be perpendicular to the cut line which acts as a frontal plane. In elevation drawing, the viewer looks directly into the object—or design—and establishes a frontal plane which is perpendicular to the sight line. Frontal plane in this kind of situation can be the facade of a building, a row of trees, or the entrance to the design. Since section shows only the profile along the cut line, the amount of recordable images can be minimal and less than interesting. Therefore, sections are sometimes replaced by section-elevation to include the images behind the cut line. This adds depth to the drawing and is after all a more interesting drawing to look at.

The most important thing to remember in section and elevation drawing is scale change. Plans drawn at small scale (1" = 50' and down, i.e., 100', 200', and so on) can still be nice and readable drawings. Sections drawn even at 1" = 40' scale can be dull and uninformative. Often section and elevation drawings have to be drawn at scale of 1" = 20' or larger, i.e., 1/16", 1/10", 1/8", or even 1/4", to be meaningful and legible. In construction documents, sections and elevations are often drawn at a very large architectural scale such as 1/2", 1 1/2", or even 3" to reveal the materials and method of construction.

Drawing type:
Elevation
Subject: Waterfront
Medium/techniques:
Pen on vellum
Original size:
11" x 8 1/2"
Source: Wang
Associates
International

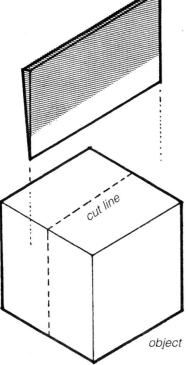

cut line

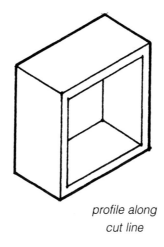

object

profile along cut line

section view

Construction detail shows the construction materials, methods of construction, and dimensioning.

Landscape shows the change in topography.

Landscape and building show the location of the house and the indoor/outdoor relationship.

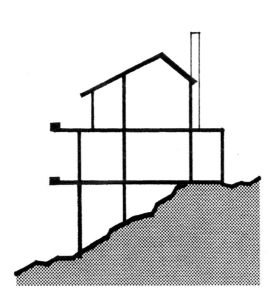

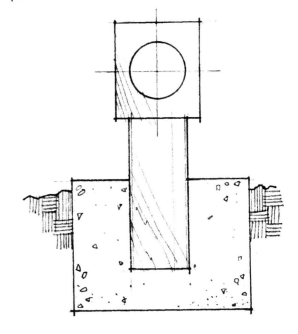

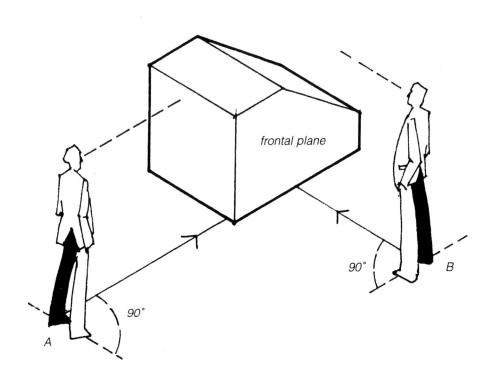

frontal plane

90°

B

90°

A

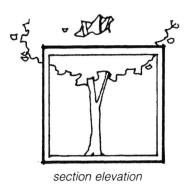

section elevation

perspective

elevations

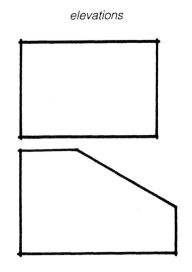

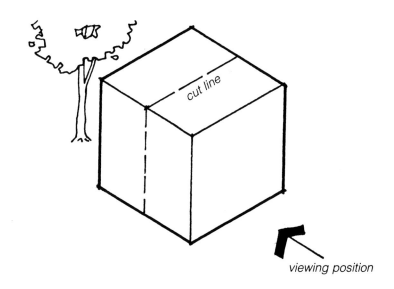

cut line

viewing position

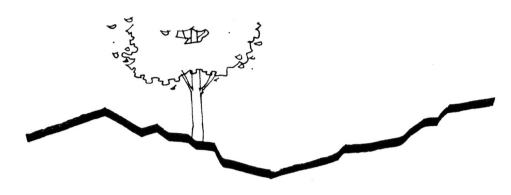

section

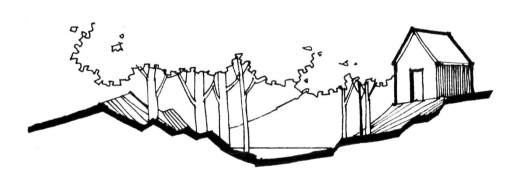

section elevation

section perspective

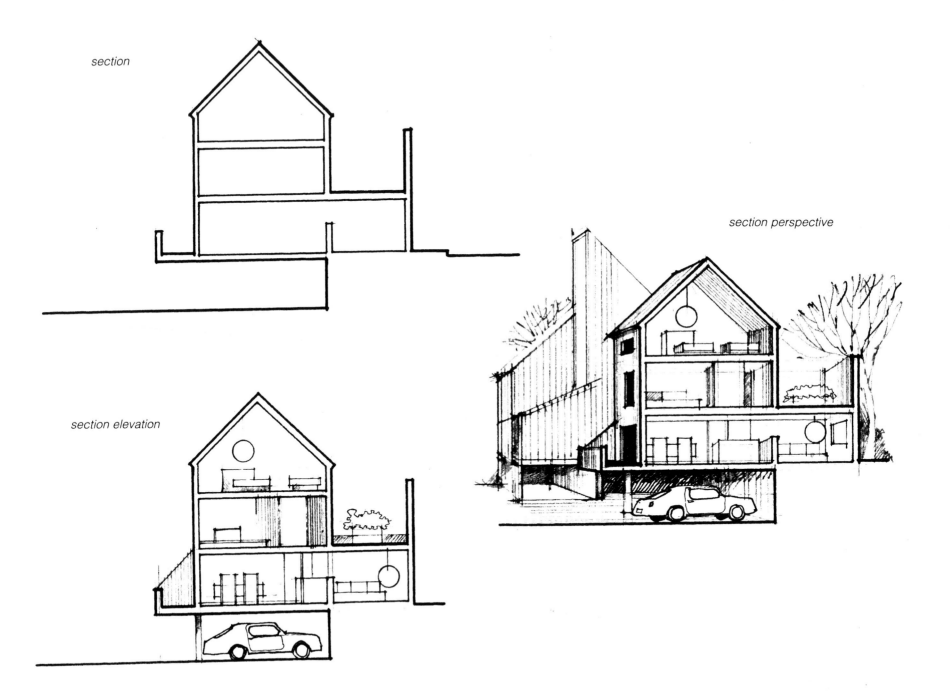

section

section perspective

section elevation

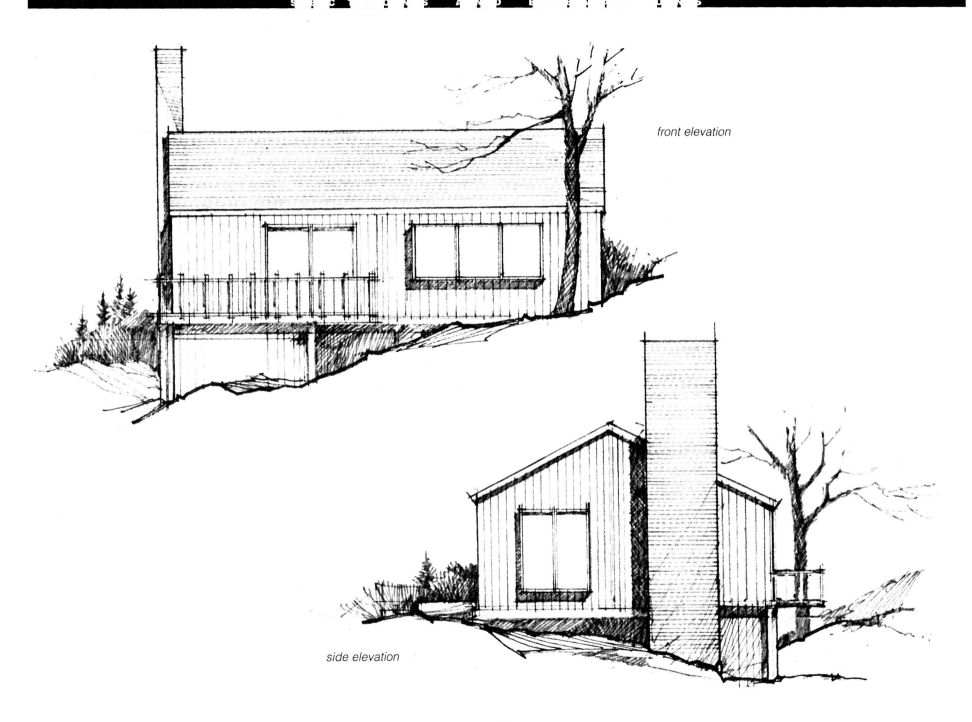

front elevation

side elevation

Vertical Exaggeration

In large landscape planning projects, section drawings are used to illustrate the variation of the topography and the relationship between valleys and ridges, land mass and water, hills and plains, and so on. Because of the vast horizontal distance which can be in miles, vertical dimensions if drawn according to the same horizontal scale will not be visible. The span of the horizontal distance is often so great that it makes the change seem insignificant. In this situation, vertical scale is exaggerated to enlarge the height and to amplify its effect. It is an incorrect projection but an effective way to communicate a simple message.

The intent of section and elevation drawings is to show the change in the vertical dimension. The span of the horizontal distance is often so great that it makes the change seem insignificant. Vertical exaggeration is used to enlarge the height in order to amplify its effect. It is a distorted image. Vertical exaggeration is frequently used in regional sections to show the relationship between subregions. It is not appropriate in man-made environments to exaggerate the vertical dimension.

no vertical exaggeration

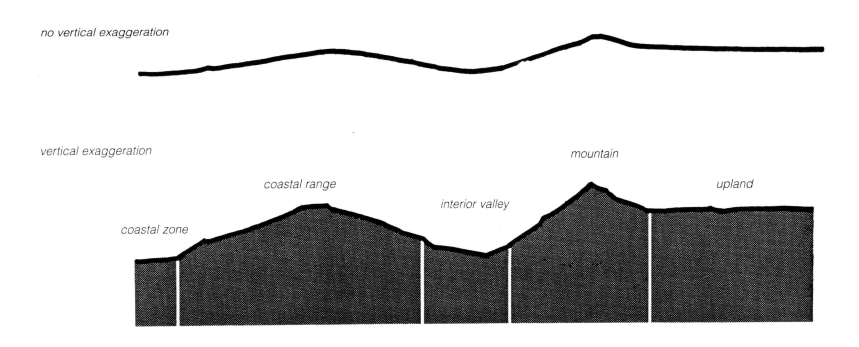

vertical exaggeration

mountain

coastal range

interior valley

upland

coastal zone

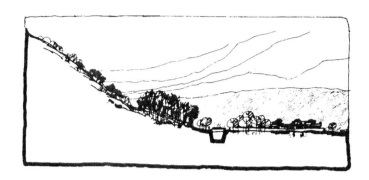

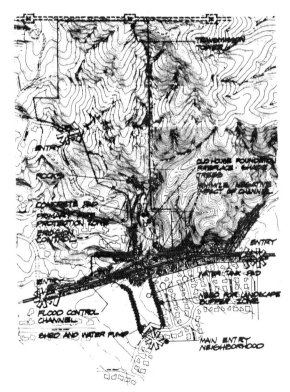

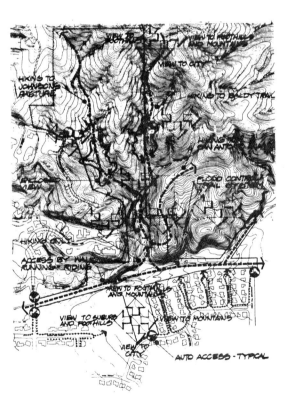

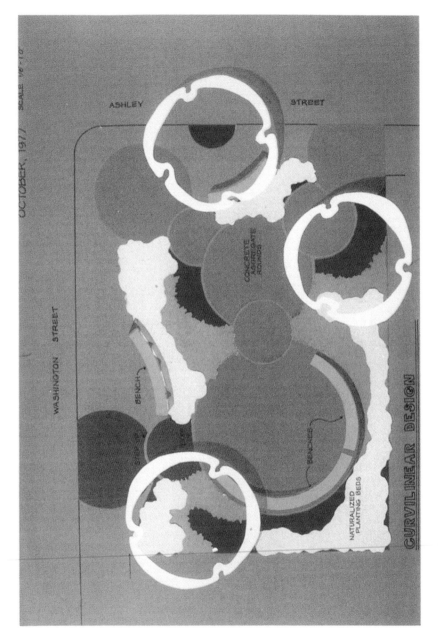

Drawing type: Plan
Subject: Urban parks
Medium/techniques: Pantone color paper
Original size: 20" x 16"
Source: Left: Student work, University of Michigan; Right: Wang Associates International

Drawing type: Plans
Subject: Room
Medium/techniques: Pantone color paper
Original size: 20" x 16"
Source: Student works, Harvard Graduate School of Design

THE CASCADES

ESTATE OF

MRS. EDITH ROCKEFELLER McCORMICK

A. W. R. MEMORIAL

Drawing type: Plans
Subject: Historical plan
Medium/techniques: Watercolor
Original size: 36" x 24"
Source: University of Illinois, Department of Landscape Architecture Archive

SECTION

Drawing type: Plan/elevations
Subject: Urban plaza
Medium/techniques: Markers on blackline print
Original size: 24" x 36"
Source: Student work, University of Michigan

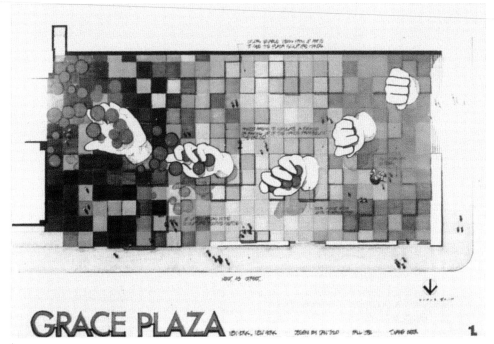

GRACE PLAZA

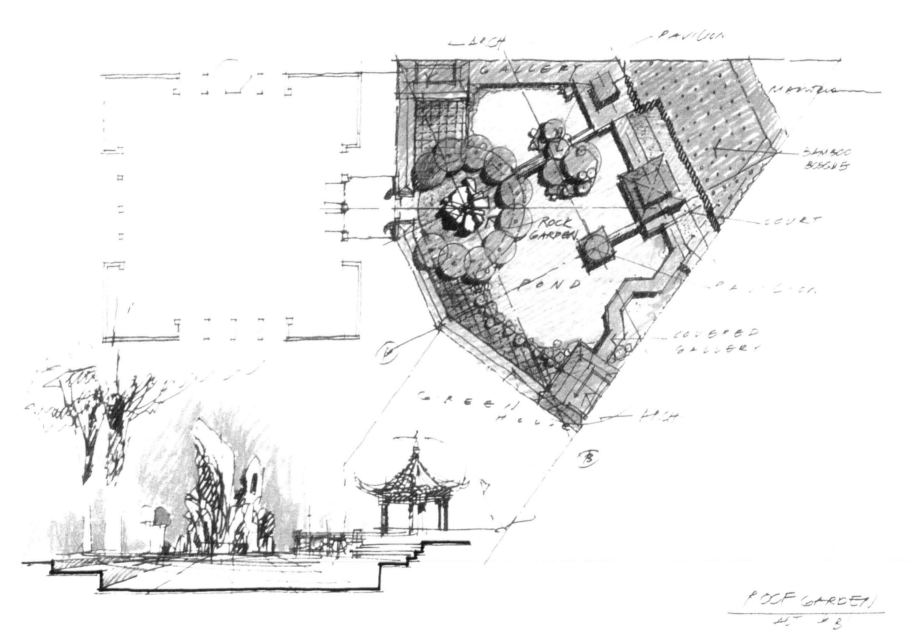

Drawing type: Plan and section perspective
Subject: Rooftop perspective
Medium/techniques: Pentel sign pen with Prismacolor pencils on white tracing paper
Original size: 24" x 24"
Source: The Stubbins Associates Inc.; Wang Associates International

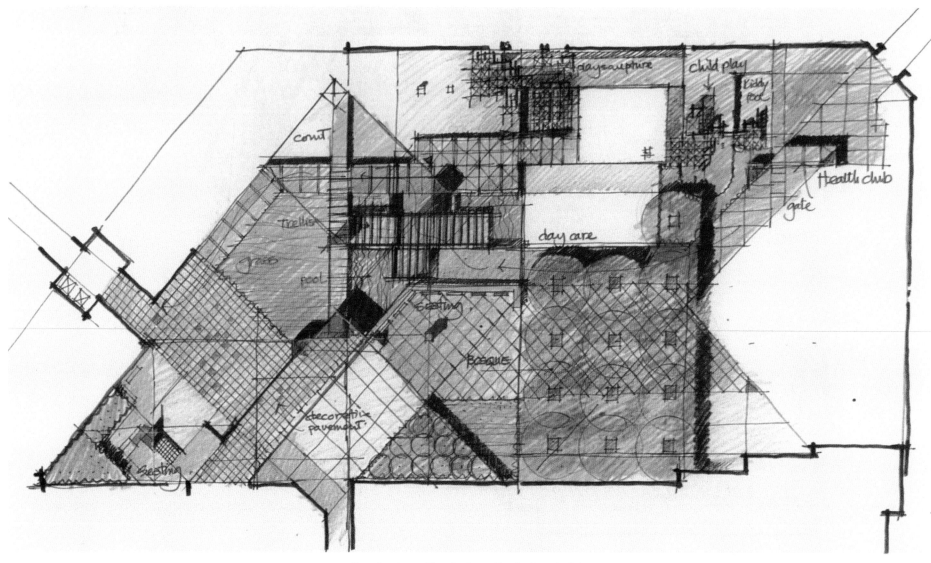

Drawing type: Plan (schematic design study)
Subject: Rooftop garden
Medium/techniques: Boldliners and Prismacolor pencils on yellow tracing paper
Original size: 14" x 24"
Source: Wang Associates International

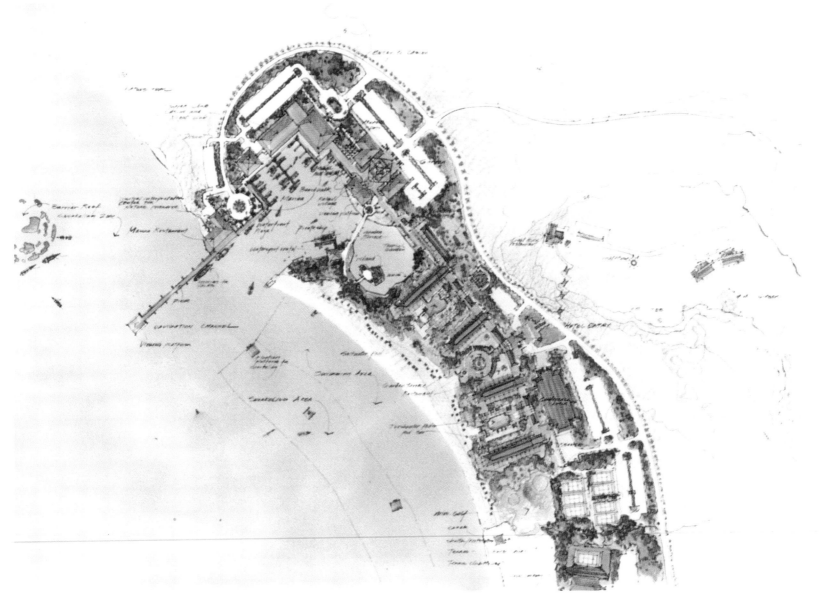

Drawing type: Plan (for presentation)
Subject: Resort
Medium/techniques: Original—boldliners on white tracing paper; full sign photographically copied on glossy photographic paper; dry mounted on rigid foam board; colored with markers and Prismacolor pencils; water done with airbrush
Original size: 30" x 42"
Source: Sasaki Associates Inc.

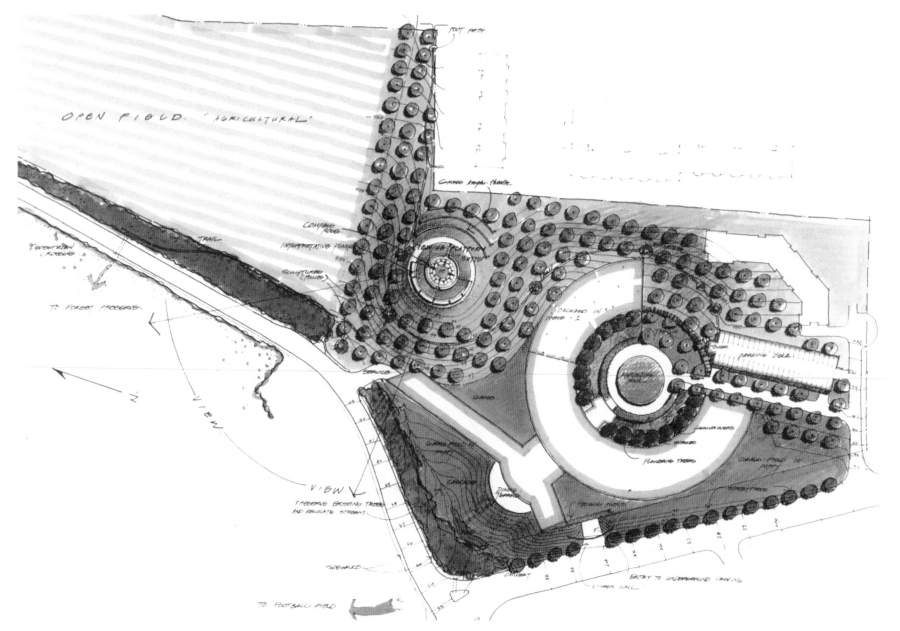

Drawing type: Plan (schematic design studies)
Subject: Bank
Medium/techniques: Colored markers on blackline print; shading done with colored pencils
Original size: 24" x 36"
Source: Wang Associates International

MASTER PLAN

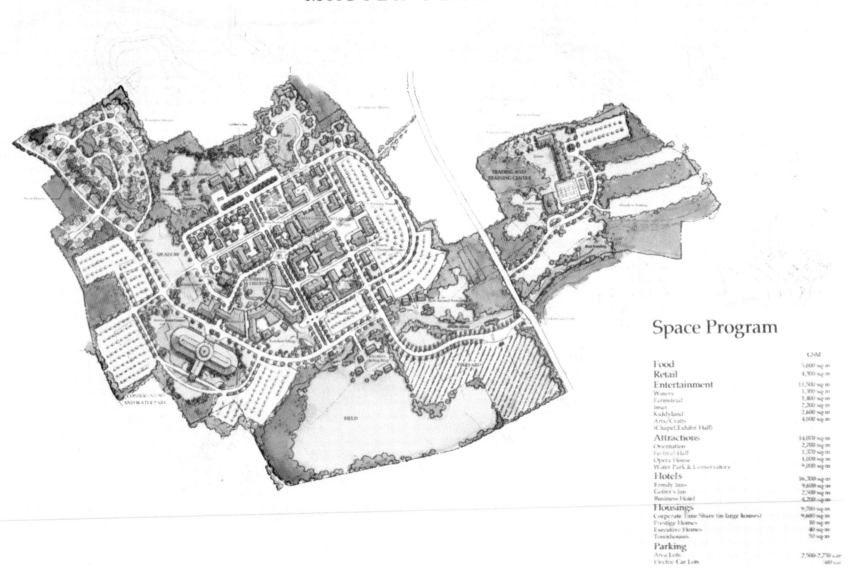

Space Program

	GSM
Food	5,000 sq m
Retail	4,700 sq m
Entertainment	11,500 sq m
Winery	1,300 sq m
Farmstead	1,400 sq m
Imax	2,200 sq m
Kiddyland	2,600 sq m
Arts/Crafts (Chapel,Exhibit Hall)	4,000 sq m
Attractions	14,070 sq m
Orientation	2,700 sq m
Festival Hall	1,370 sq m
Opera House	1,000 sq m
Water Park & Conservatory	9,000 sq m
Hotels	16,300 sq m
Family Inns	9,600 sq m
Golfer's Inn	2,500 sq m
Business Hotel	4,200 sq m
Housings	9,780 sq m
Corporate Time Share (in large houses)	9,680 sq m
Prestige Homes	10 sq m
Executive Homes	40 sq m
Townhouses	50 sq m
Parking	
Area Lots	2,500-2,750 car
Electric Car Lots	400 car

Drawing type: Plan (for presentation)
Subject: Resort
Medium/techniques: Original—boldliners on white tracing paper; large format copy on presentation paper
(watercolor paper equivalent); drymounted on rigid foam board; illustrated with watercolor
Original size: AO 30" x 48"
Source: Sasaki Associates Inc.

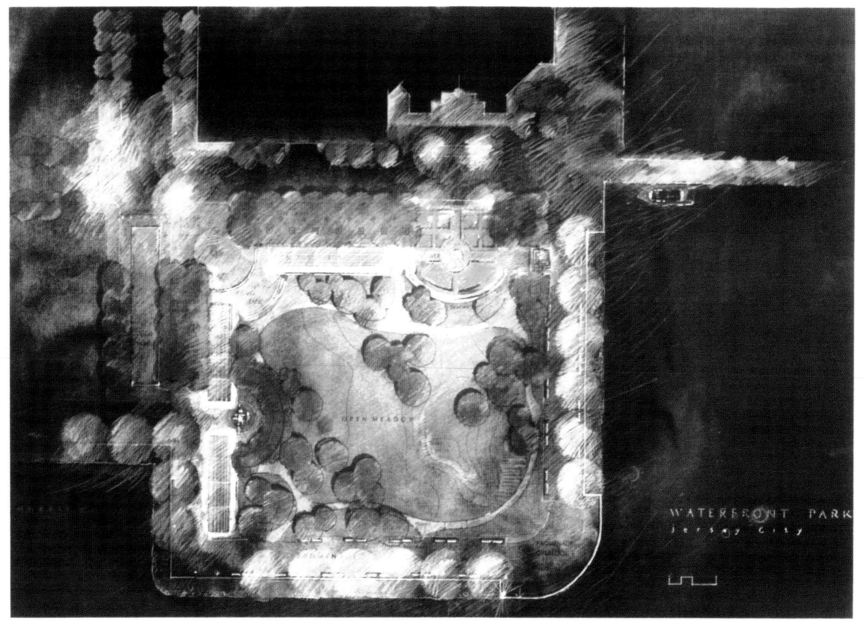

Drawing type: Plan (for presentation)
Subject: Waterfront park
Medium/techniques: Prismacolor pencils on standard blackline print with dark background; water done with airbrush (black ink)
Original size: 18" x 24"
Source: Sasaki Associates Inc.

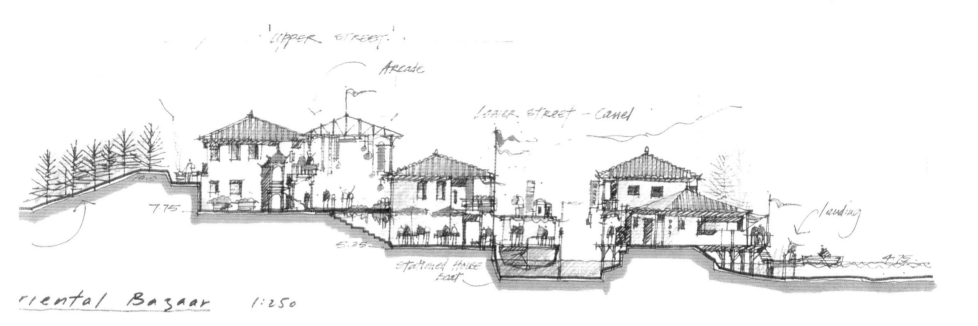

upper street

arcade

lower street – canal

landing

7.75

5.25

stationed house boat

riental Bazaar   1:250

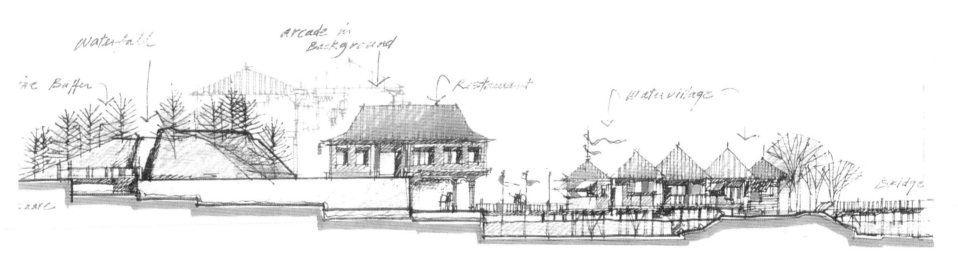

waterfall

arcade in background

restaurant

water village

ive buffer

bridge

Drawing type: Section/elevation
Subject: Waterfront festival market
Medium/techniques: Black and brown razorpoint with colored pencils; profile line outlined with markers
Original size: 12" x 24"
Source: Wang Associates International

BASE CAMP (OUTWARD BOUND)
SECTION.

APPROACH

POOL ON DECK

BLDG. ON DECK. W/
CONC. PILLARS!

VIEW

BUILT-IN ROCK
CLIMBING TRAINING
CENTER ON
CONC. PILLARS &
WALLS

ENTRY VIA
BRIDGE

EAST & NORTH SLOPE.
ROPE CLIMBING COURSE

180
170
160
150
140
130
120 — m.

0   10   30 m.

Drawing type: Section/elevation
Subject: Hillside Development
Medium/techniques: Black boldliner with colored markers on white
paper, highlight with red boldliner
Original size: Left, 12" x 24"; Bottom, 12" x 16"
Source: Sasaki Associates Inc.

90
80
70
60
METER 50

PPTY
Line

Aquatic exhibits.

animal exhibits.

PLAZA

EL. 57

upper level: adm.
lower level: displays

TROPICAL
RAIN FOREST
+ Displays
(CENTRAL PAVILION)

RET. WALL
periscope alley

LOWER ACTIVITY CORE : SECTION-ELEVATION

1:250

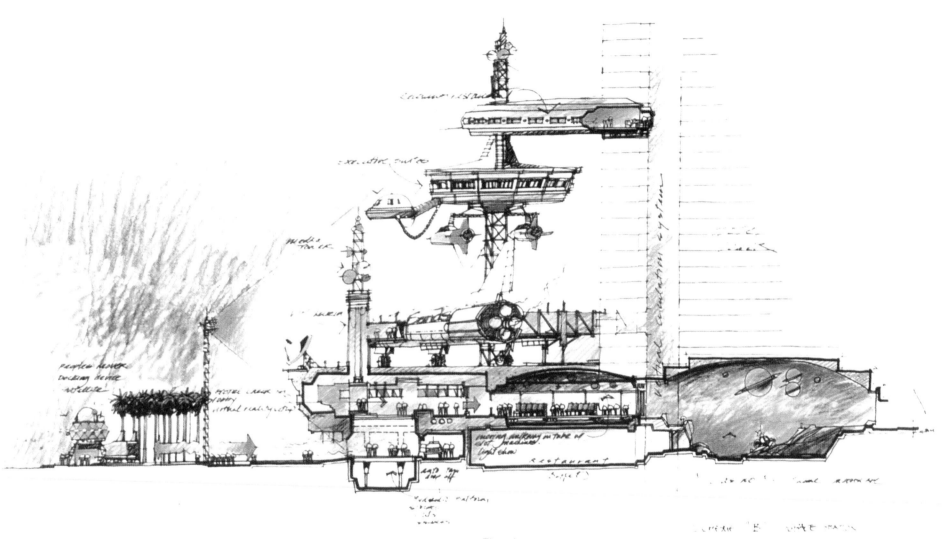

Drawing type: Elevation
Subject: Theme entertainment
Medium/techniques: Pentel sign pen and Prismacolor pencils on white tracing paper
Original size: 18" x 30"
Source: Wang Associates International; The Stubbins Associates Inc.

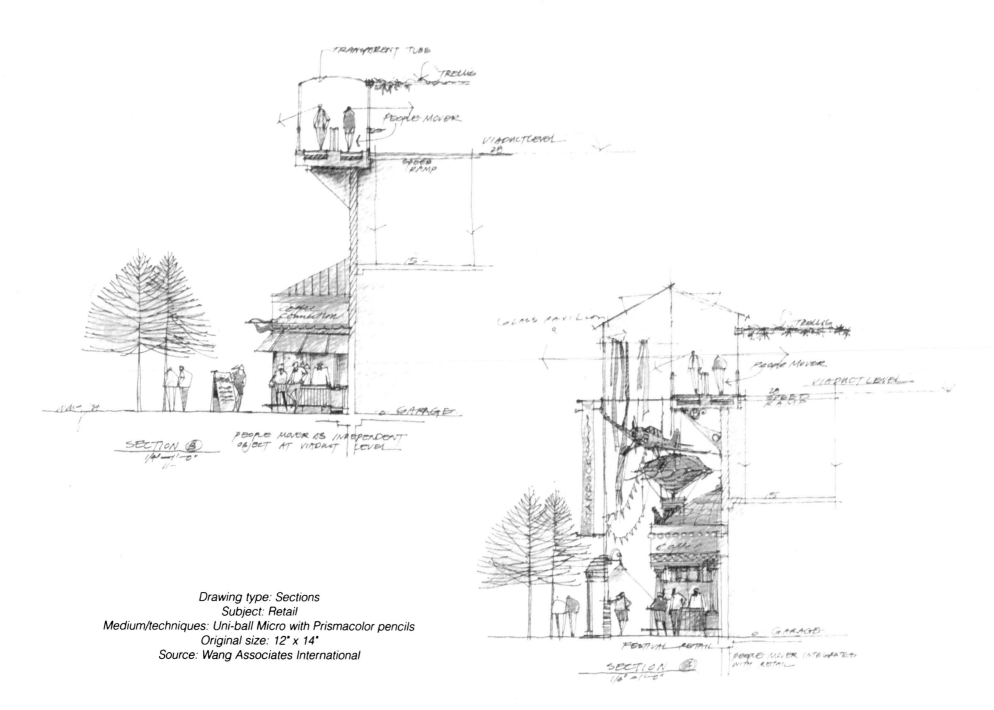

TRANSPARENT TUBE

TRELLIS

PEOPLE MOVER

VIADUCT LEVEL 2B

SPEED RAMP

15

Coffee Connection

GARAGE

SECTION B
1/4" = 1'-0"

PEOPLE MOVER AS INDEPENDENT OBJECT AT VIADUCT LEVEL

GLASS PAVILION

TRELLIS

PEOPLE MOVER

VIADUCT LEVEL

SPEED RAMP

15

Cafe

GARAGE

FESTIVAL RETAIL

PEOPLE MOVER INTEGRATED WITH RETAIL

SECTION A
1/4" = 1'-0"

Drawing type: Sections
Subject: Retail
Medium/techniques: Uni-ball Micro with Prismacolor pencils
Original size: 12" x 14"
Source: Wang Associates International

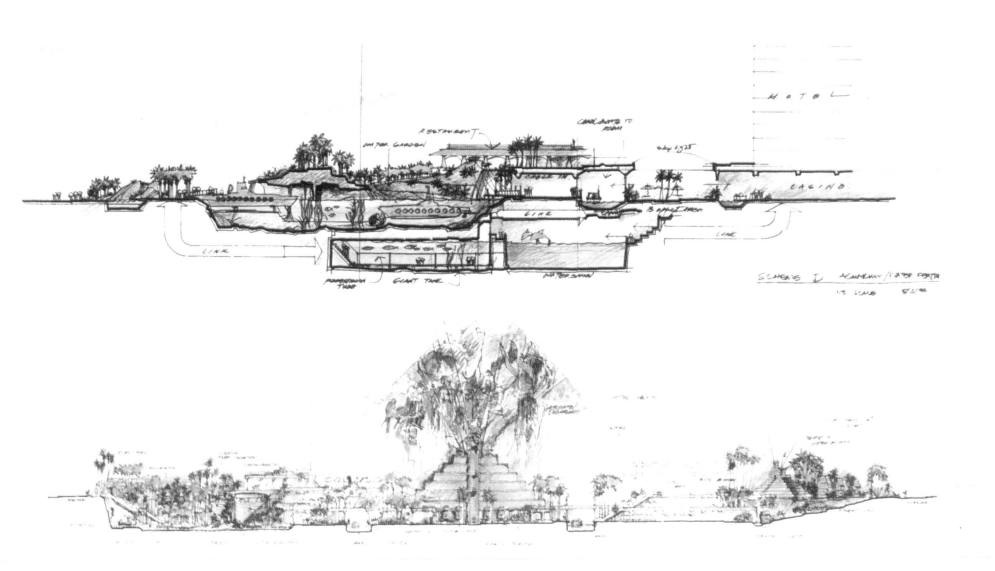

Subject: Casino themes
Medium/techniques: Pentel sign pen with Prismacolor pencils on white tracing paper
Original size: 14" x 36"
Source: Wang Associates International; The Stubbins Associates Inc.

Drawing type: Section/elevation
Subject: Hillside condominium development
Medium/techniques: Razorpoint and colored markers on white tracing paper
Original size: 12" x 24"
Source: Sasaki Associates Inc.

Section Graphics

Graphic Vocabulary

Graphic vocabulary in section and elevation drawings can be classified into four major groups: architecture, vegetation, design features, and supporting elements. Unlike plan drawings which require abstract and stylized symbols, graphic vocabulary in section and elevation drawings includes images that resemble the real things.

Drawing type: Schematic section
Subject: Retail village
Medium/techniques: Berol boldliner and colored markers on white tracing paper
Original size: 36" x 18"
Source: Sasaki Associates Inc.

Architecture

Section and elevation information on architectural subjects can be obtained from the architects' drawings. Depending on the design intent, these drawings can be transferred or redrawn to incorporate landscape treatments and other landscape design features in front. If the intent of the elevation is to show the street trees in front of the building, the architectural elevation can be simplified to highlight the trees. On the other hand, if the intent is to show off the architecture, the trees in front of the building would have to be more abstract and drawn with less details.

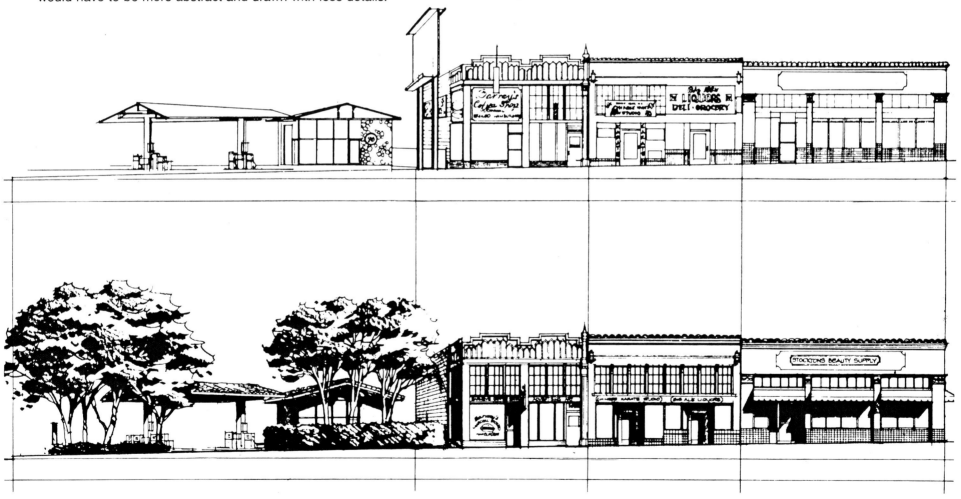

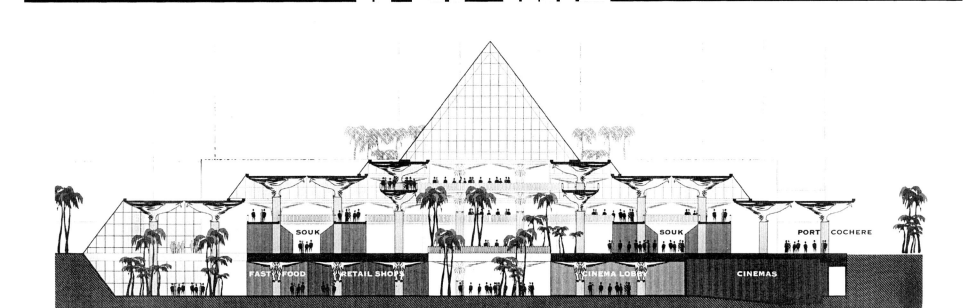

Above:
Drawing type: Section
Subject: Retail
Medium/techniques: Computer-generated
Original size: 24" x 18"
Source: D'Agostino Izzo Quirk Architects

Below:
Drawing type: Elevation
Subject: Housing
Medium/techniques: Pencil on vellum
Original size: 24" x 16"
Source: Wang Associates International

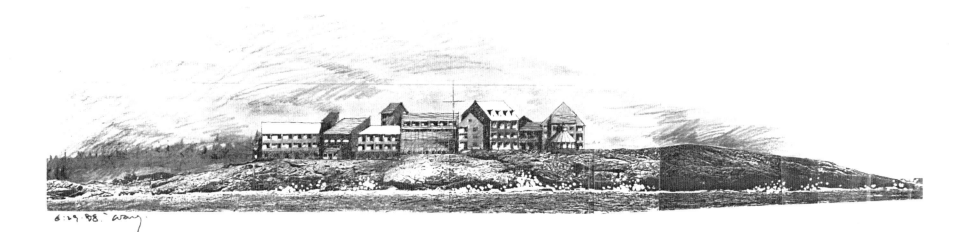

Vegetation

Vegetation is the most important element in section and elevation drawings. Since plant materials in side view are a lot more complicated than their counterparts in plan drawings, the designer must understand the various tree forms and the ways to graphically portray them. Instead of drawing repetitive circles in plan drawing, plant materials in section and elevation drawings must be drawn specifically to indicate the species, branching style, age, and foliage of each plant. This means that the designer must understand the basic tree forms and the way they grow.

For example, the branching pattern of an upright tree such as pin oak is very different from willow which is more irregular with soft arching branches. Evergreens such as white pine have a very different kind of foliage than that of a spruce. These differences in form, branching style, and foliage are very important in landscape design and therefore should not be treated indiscriminatory in section and elevation drawings. The best way to understand these differences is to assemble a photographic album or sketchbook of trees and shrubs to be used as a reference.

There are many ways to draw trees but the most effective way is to first define the outline of a tree with simple lines. The trunks of trees must be drawn first because the trunks dictate the spacing between trees. Lines pulling away from the trunk define the branches. Stipples or scribbles of lines can be used to indicate foliage and to fill in the canopy.

ways to draw trees

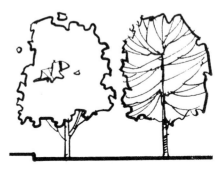

outline   outline and branch

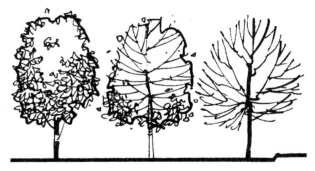

texture   texture and outline   branch

basic tree forms

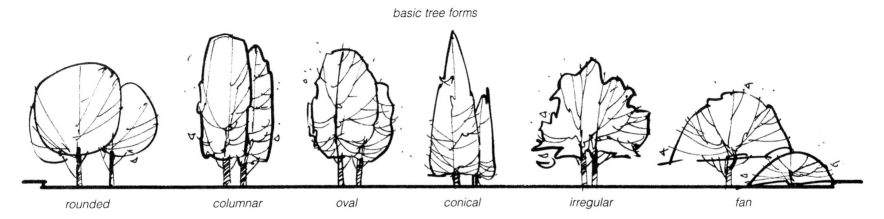

rounded   columnar   oval   conical   irregular   fan

104

plan view

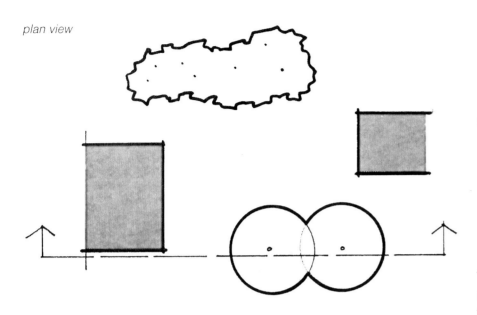

elevation

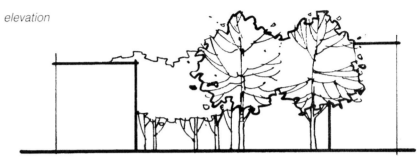

Trees in the background are drawn with a thin line. They are on the same scale as the rest of the frontal plane because it is an orthographic projection.

plan view

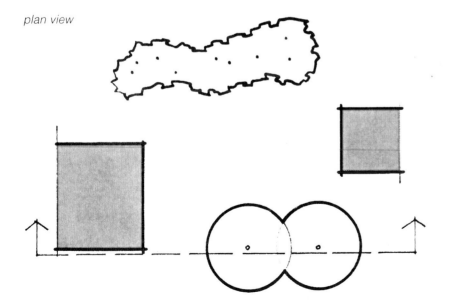

perspective

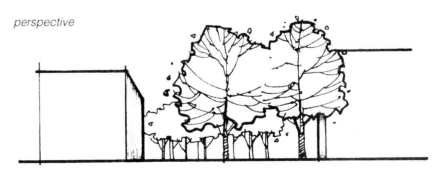

Background trees are smaller because of the perspective image.

examples of deciduous trees

examples of evergreen trees

examples of foreground trees

These symbols are for framing. The trees in the foreground should have more detail. The outline of close-up materials should be drawn with a thick line.

how to draw trees

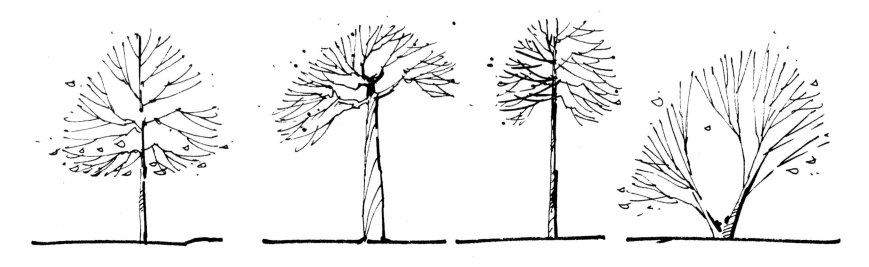

typical branch-type tree symbols

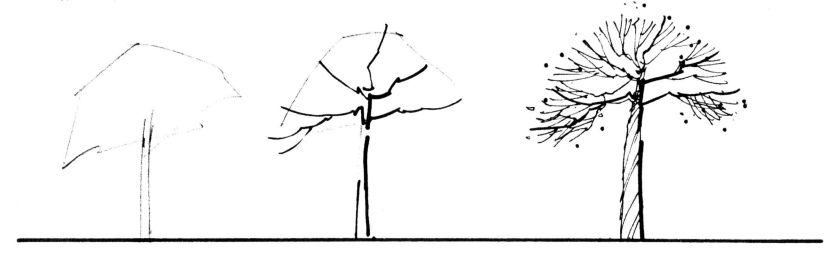

Outline the tree with a thin pencil line. Sketch the major branches and reinforce the trunk. Fill in the rest of the branches. Add a few stipples as an indication of motion.

The technique of drawing shrubs is similar to that of trees. A combination of outlines and branches is the most effective shrub symbol. Textures should be used to represent foliage and ground covers.

basic shrub forms

oval, rounded   *fan*   *low, creeping*   *lawn*

outline and branch

texture

texture

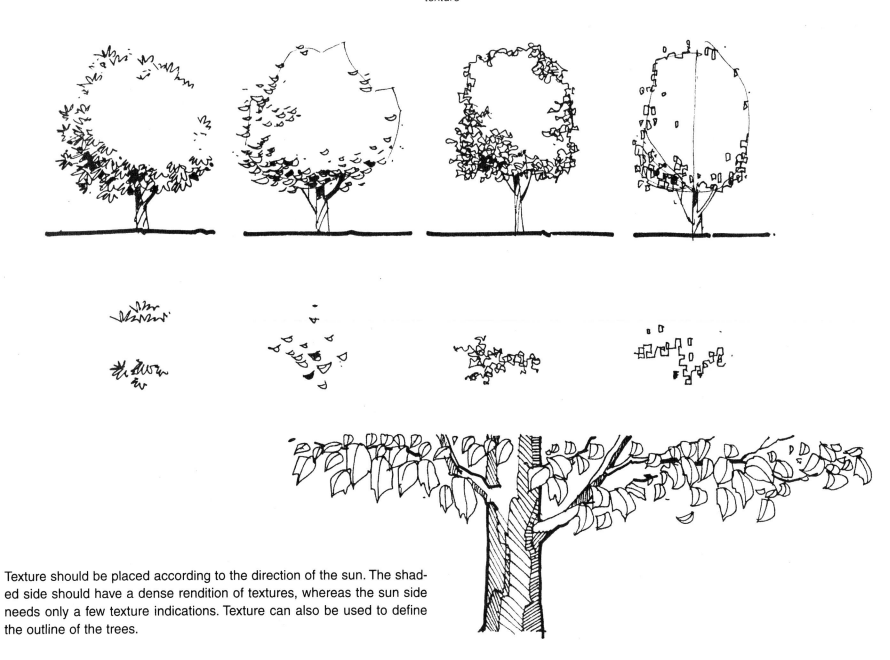

Texture should be placed according to the direction of the sun. The shaded side should have a dense rendition of textures, whereas the sun side needs only a few texture indications. Texture can also be used to define the outline of the trees.

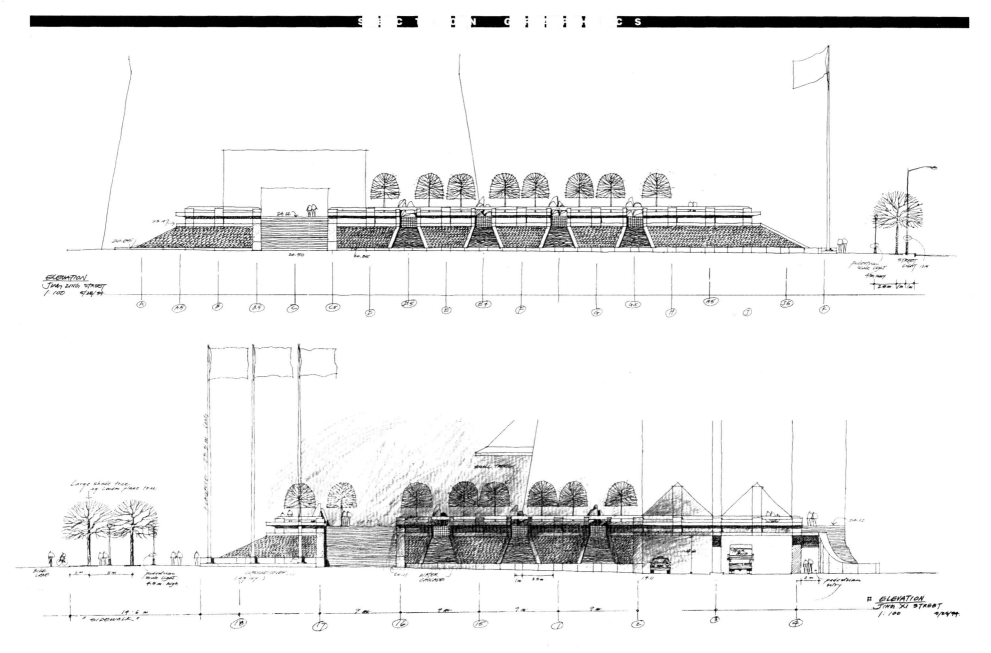

Drawing type: Elevation
Subject: Plaza
Medium/techniques: Berol boldliner on white tracing paper. Colored with Prismacolor pencils.
Source: Wang Associates International; The Stubbins Associates Inc.

Human Figures

Human figures are very important features in section and elevation drawings. When put next to other design elements, figures humanize the design and evoke scale comparison. Figures should be drawn similar to the scale of the accompanying section or elevation. The placement and quantity of figures should be part of the overall composition. The intent of figures is to support the design; they should not become the center of attention. Therefore figures in section and elevation drawings should be carefully selected to match the design subject and to coincide with the sit-

uation. The choices of clothing, age, gender, and activities are all important decisions which must be made when putting human figures in sections and elevations. A very useful resource is to compile a figure file from magazines and photographs. These figure cutouts can be easily enlarged or reduced to fit the scale of the drawing. This practice helps to introduce a sense of reality to the drawing and can make an otherwise mundane section or elevation drawing more lively.

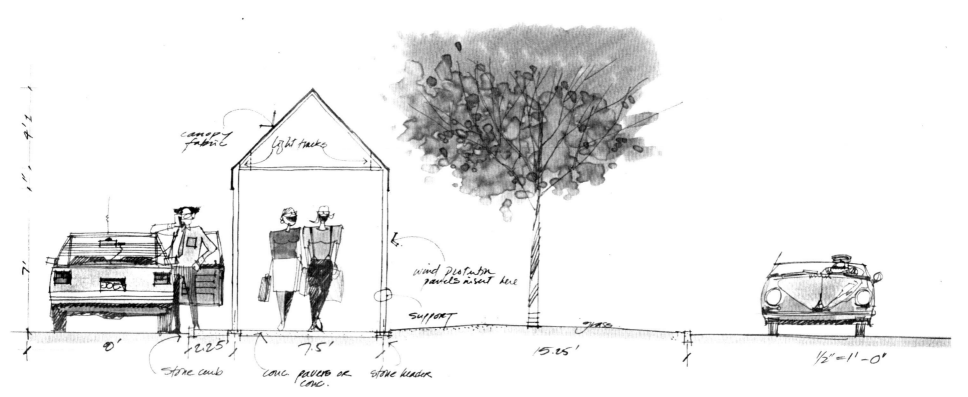

Drawing type: Section/elevation
Subject: Parking lot
Medium/techniques: Berol boldliners and colored markers
Original size: 14" x 24"
Source: Wang Associates International

Drawing type: Elevation
Subject: Aquarium entrance
Medium/techniques: Berol boldliner and colored markers on white tracing paper
Original size: 18" x 24"
Source: Sasaki Associates Inc.

Ground

Ground is insignificant in section and elevation drawings because it can only be expressed as a thick profile line. In order to show more explicit change along the profile line, a base is sometimes added below the profile line to establish a heavier baseline and therefore emphasize contrast.

Section and elevation are two-dimensional drawings. They do not show perspective and therefore do not give the viewer the illusion of depth. Varying line widths are the key to depth reference in section and elevation drawings. The cut line is usually the thickest line because it is the closest to the viewer. Heavy lines give the drawing a steady foundation. Objects in the distance should be drawn with thinner lines, but the profile of these objects should be outlined with a medium line for better definition. Zip-a-tone is often used to mask a consistent base for all section and elevation drawings despite the variation on the surface.

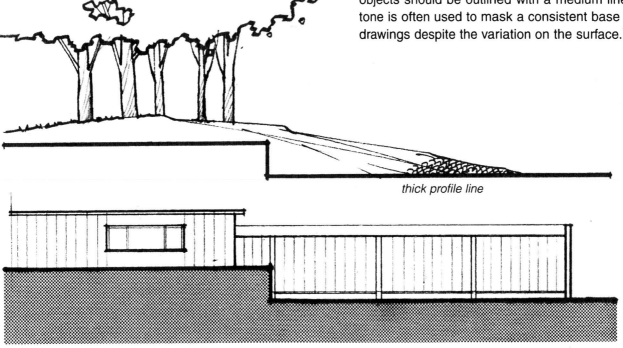

thick profile line

Zip-a-tone

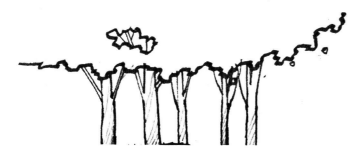

Zip-a-tone

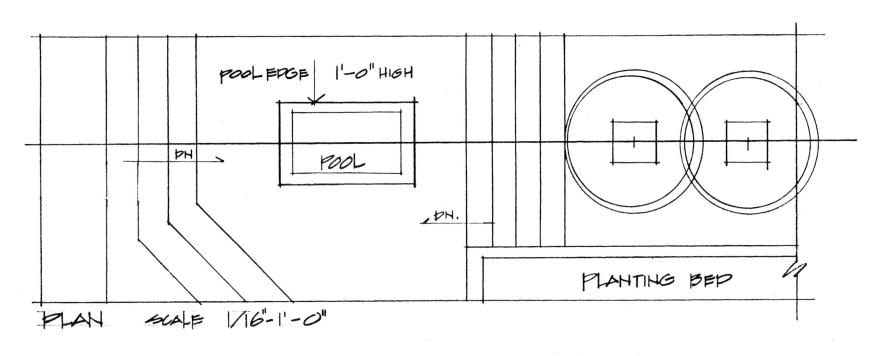

POOL EDGE | 1'-0" HIGH

POOL

PLANTING BED

PLAN   SCALE 1/16"-1'-0"

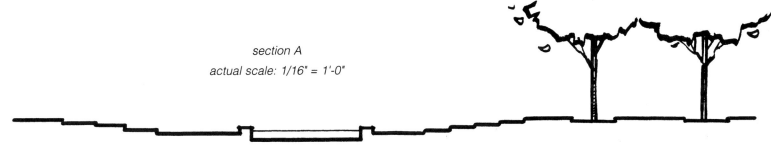

section A
actual scale: 1/16" = 1'-0"

section B   vertical scale: 1/8" = 1'-0"
V.E. = 2:1   horizontal scale: 1/16" = 1'-0"

Drawing type: Elevation
Subject: Waterfront development
Medium/techniques: Pencil on white tracing paper
Original size: 36" x 48"
Source: Sasaki Associates Inc.

Annotations

Section and elevation drawings often must rely on annotations to clarify the message. Annotations should be preplanned during the layout of the drawing and should never be done as an afterthought. Text should be organized, consistent, and simple. Selection of fonts and the size of letters should be designed to fit into the entire composition.

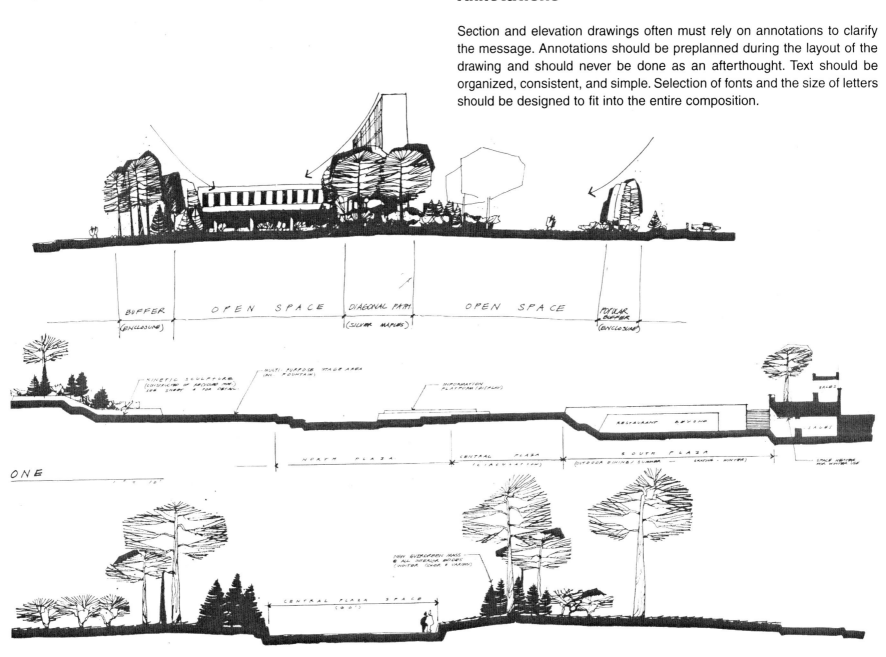

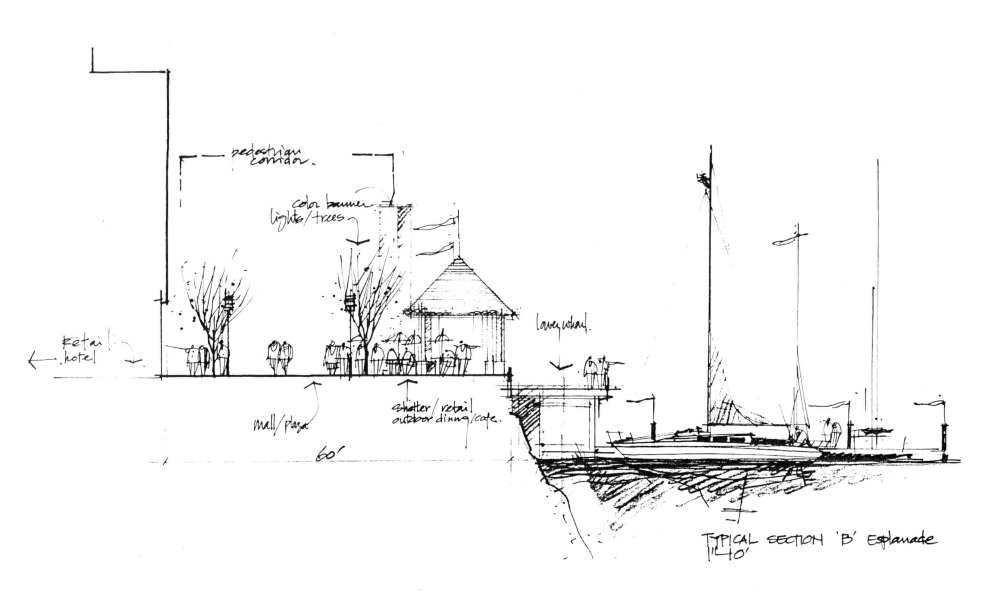

pedestrian corridor.

color banner

lights/trees

Retail
.hotel

Mall/plaza

60'

Shelter/retail
outdoor dining/cafe.

lower wharf.

TYPICAL SECTION 'B' Esplanade
1"=40'

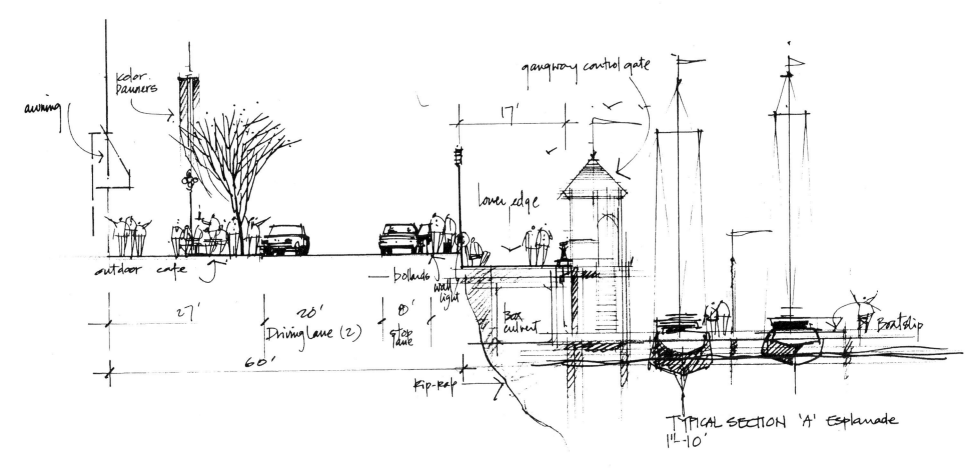

awning

Kolor. Banners

outdoor cafe

27'

20'
Driving Lane (2)

60'

8'
stop
lane

bollards

wall
light

Box
culvert

Rip-Rap

gangway control gate

17'

lower edge

Boat slip

TYPICAL SECTION 'A' Esplanade
1"L=10'

Facing Pages:
Drawing type: Section/elevation
Subject: Waterfront esplanade
Medium/techniques: Pencils and Berol boldliners on white tracing paper
Original size: 11" x 17"
Source: Wang Associates International

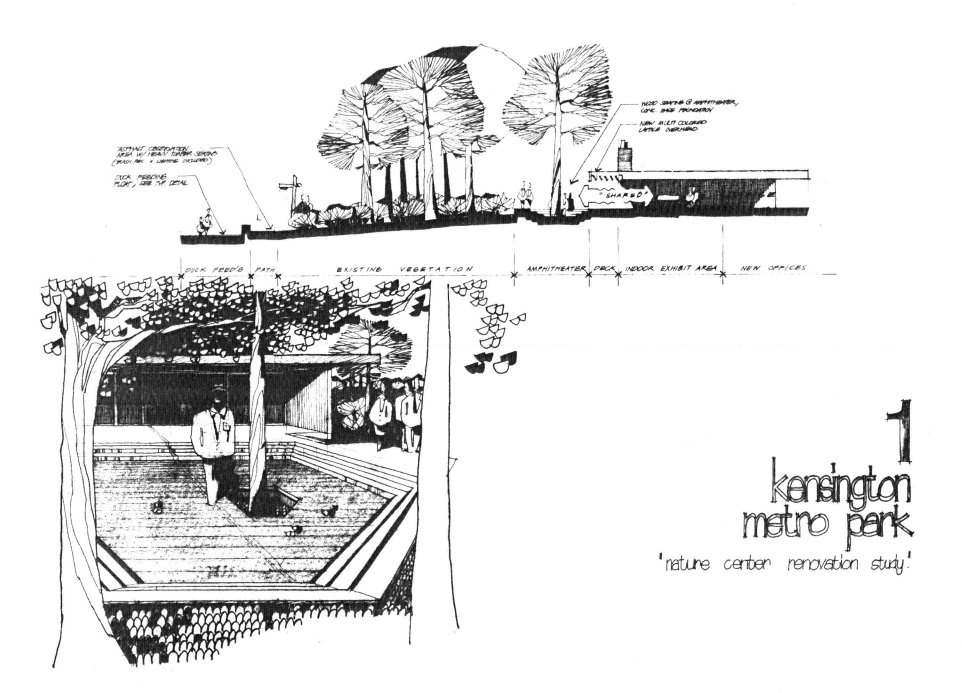

ASPHALT OBSERVATION
AREA W/ HEAVY TIMBER SEATING
(TRASH REC + LIGHTING INCLUDED)

DUCK FEEDING
FLOAT, SEE TYP. DETAIL

WOOD SEATING @ AMPHITHEATER,
CONC. BASE FOUNDATION

NEW MULTI COLORED
LATTICE OVERHEAD

"SHARED"

DUCK FEED'G PATH   EXISTING   VEGETATION   AMPHITHEATER DECK   INDOOR EXHIBIT AREA   NEW OFFICES

1
kensington
metro park
'nature center renovation study!'

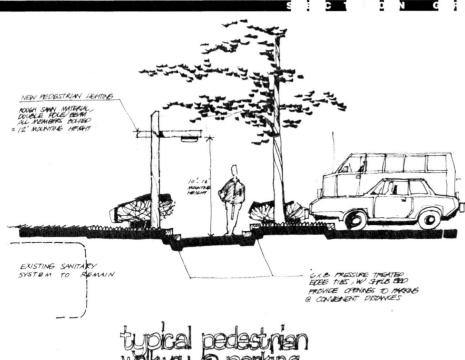

NEW PEDESTRIAN LIGHTING

ROUGH SAWN MATERIAL, DOUBLE POLE/BEAM ALL MEMBERS BOLTED ± 12' MOUNTING HEIGHT

10'-12 MOUNTING HEIGHT

EXISTING SANITARY SYSTEM TO REMAIN.

6 x 8 PRESSURE TREATED EDGE TIES, W/ SHRUB BED PROVIDE OPENINGS TO PARKING @ CONVENIENT DISTANCES

typical pedestrian walkway @ parking

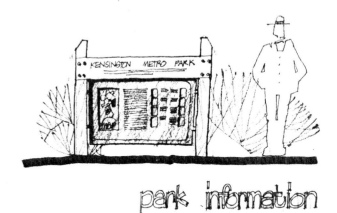

KENSINGTON METRO PARK

park information

2
kensington metro park

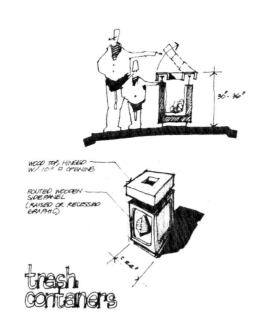

30"-36"

WOOD TOP, HINGED W/ 10" □ OPENING

ROUTED WOODEN SIDE PANEL (RAISED OR RECESSED GRAPHIC)

trash containers

ROUTED WOODEN TRAIL IDENTIFICATION MARKER, RAISED OR RECESSED GRAPHIC, PRESERVATIVE STAIN OR EMPLOY COLOR IDENTIFICATION.

DIRECTIONAL INDICATOR OR PODED INFO

trail signage

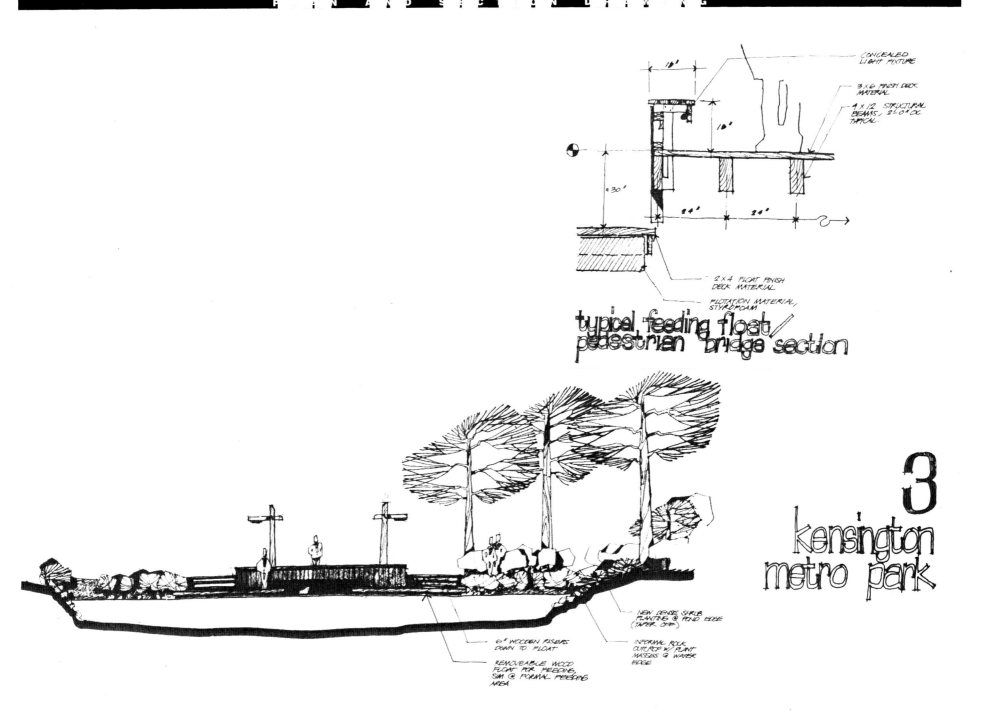

CONCEALED
LIGHT FIXTURE

3 X 6 FINISH DECK
MATERIAL

4 X 12 STRUCTURAL
BEAMS, 2'-0" O.C.
TYPICAL.

2 X 4 FLOAT FINISH
DECK MATERIAL

FLOTATION MATERIAL,
STYROFOAM

typical feeding float/
pedestrian bridge section

3
kensington
metro park

NEW DENSE SHRUB
PLANTING @ POND EDGE
(TAPER OFF)

6" WOODEN RISERS
DOWN TO FLOAT

INFORMAL ROCK
OUTCROP W/ PLANT
MASSES @ WATER
EDGE

REMOVEABLE WOOD
FLOAT FOR FEEDING,
SIM @ FORMAL FEEDING
AREA.

Computer Graphics

It is inevitable that this book must address the subject of computer graphics and its impact on contemporary plan and section drawings. Using a computer to assist in the design and graphic making processes is standard practice in almost all design offices. The term "Autocad" is almost synonymous to the production of any type of design document, and computer graphics has quickly evolved to become a mainstream subject in design education. There is no doubt that we've benefited greatly from this kind of technological advancement. We now have accurate data-base information that can easily be retrieved and transformed according to our desire. We can generate numerous design alternatives at a flick of our fingertips, all at a fraction of the time it took to do the work by hand. This kind of technological breakthrough is welcoming and exciting.

The making of a plan and section drawing must respond to these changes as design professionals have already done in many ways. The most important application is the production of construction documents (see Page 124). Design layouts and details can easily be expressed in plans or sections accompanied by consistent dimensions and annotations. Many design development drawings are drawn and updated with "Autocad." Perhaps the only areas where computer graphics have yet to gain a stronghold are the analytical and conceptual diagramming phases. Due to the random and spontaneous approach to this kind of idea tracking, designers habitually find diagramming by hand a more direct and fluid response to the impulses and signals generated and received from the mind. The lack of standards and graphic conventions in analytical and conceptual drawings also make it impossible to develop a generalized pattern of graphic expressions that can be utilized efficiently with computer graphic logic. The figure on page 125 is an attempt to graphically express the spatial relationship of a design.

Because of the way the graphic data is stored, processed, and recognized, standard geometric forms with orthogonal or circular relationships often appear more eye-pleasing than the organic shapes (see Page 126). In landscape architectural drawings where vegetation and topography play key roles in the shaping of designed spaces, the computer-generated tree images are often stiff and less life-like (see Page 127 and 128). The graphic effects of trees in a computer-generated plan or section drawing depend largely on the variety of tree symbols that are available in the system (see Page 129). These symbols are often the stylized graphic images generated and recorded by the designer. Perhaps the visual quality of these images is largely effected by the ability of the designer doing the input.

Certain computer systems may also limit the quantity of these tree symbols or may prevent the input of a more accurate portrayal of trees due to the size of the files. A realistic image of tree—for example, a photograph of a tree or a series of tree images—can be scanned and stored in the computer system. However, scanned images tend to take up a great deal of memory and hence require a more powerful computer and printer. These upgrades are advantageous if cost is not a factor. There is no question that computer graphic images can be made life-like, but at a cost.

It may be an overly simplified statement, but I do believe the key to good computer-generated imaging lies in the eyes and minds of the designer who operates the computer. The ability to visually judge an image is not a skill that can be learned overnight, but instead out of personal artistic experience that must be acquired over time. This kind of artistic skill comes from many hours of seeing and drawing by hand. It also includes understanding the basic principles of design and aesthetic. Technology will always be available for those who want to translate and reapply that knowledge and skill with the help of a computer. Nevertheless, the ability to visually diagnose and improve a drawing outweighs the need for computer graphics.

Drawing type: Section
Subject: Deck design detail
Medium/techniques: Autocad output
Source: The Stubbins Associates Inc.

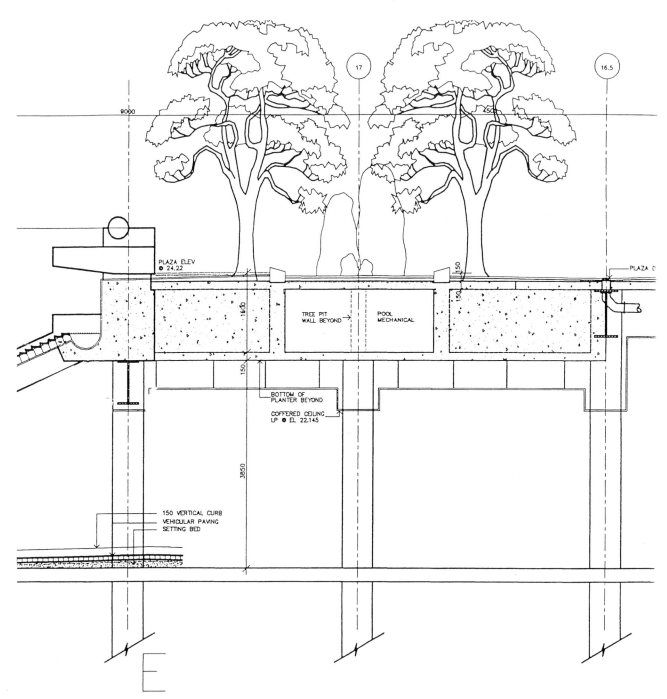

PLAZA ELEV
⊕ 24.22

TREE PIT
WALL BEYOND →   POOL
MECHANICAL

BOTTOM OF
PLANTER BEYOND

COFFERED CEILING
LP ⊕ EL 22.145

150 VERTICAL CURB
VEHICULAR PAVING
SETTING BED

PLAZA

17

16.5

124

Interzone Linkage

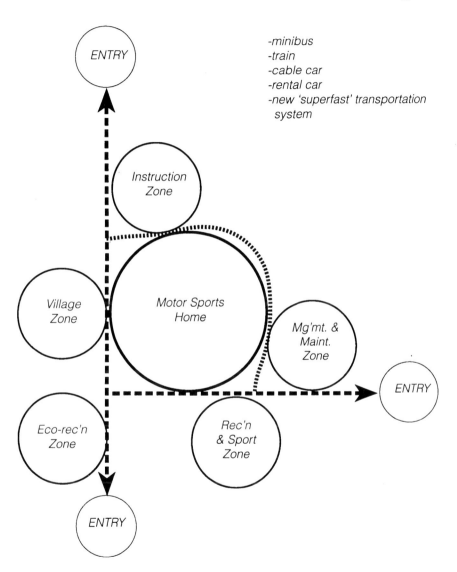

-minibus
-train
-cable car
-rental car
-new 'superfast' transportation
 system

Drawing type: Spatial relationship and linkage diagram
Subject: Motor racing center
Medium/techniques: Mac-based computer graphic
Source: Wang Associates International

Spacial Relationship & Interzone Linkage

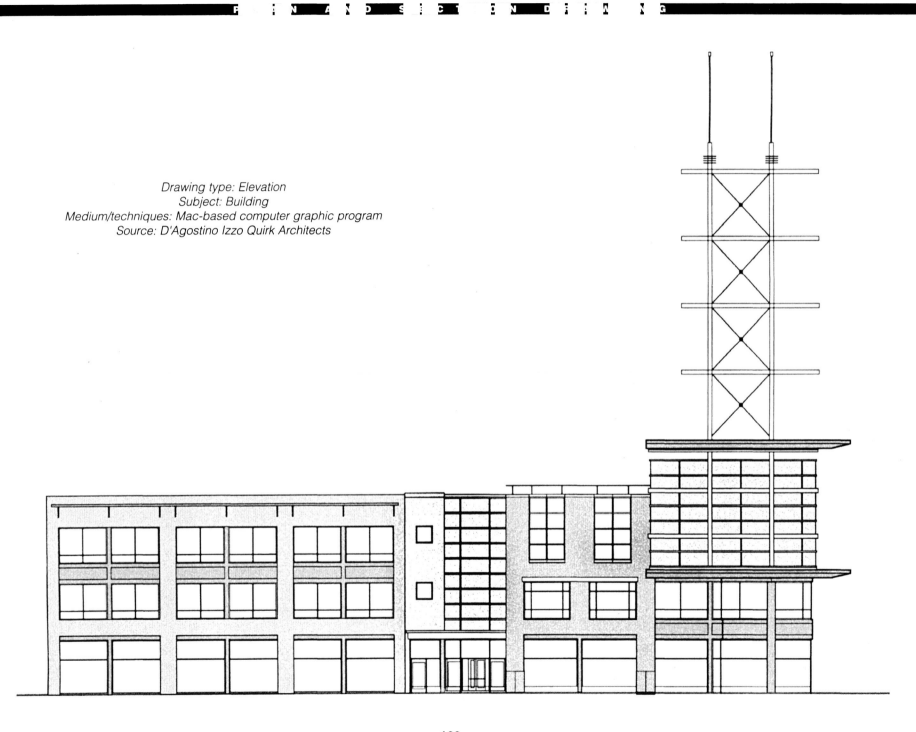

Drawing type: Elevation
Subject: Building
Medium/techniques: Mac-based computer graphic program
Source: D'Agostino Izzo Quirk Architects

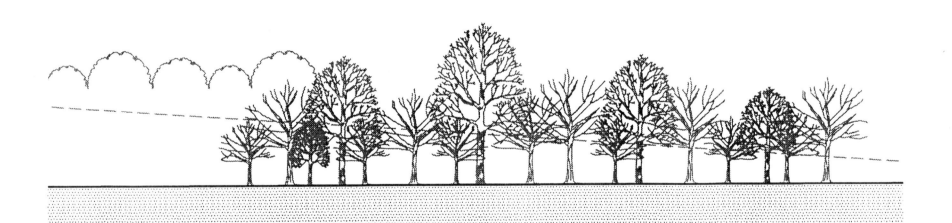

Drawing type: Section
Subject: Trees
Medium/techniques: Autocad output
Source: The Stubbins Associates Inc.

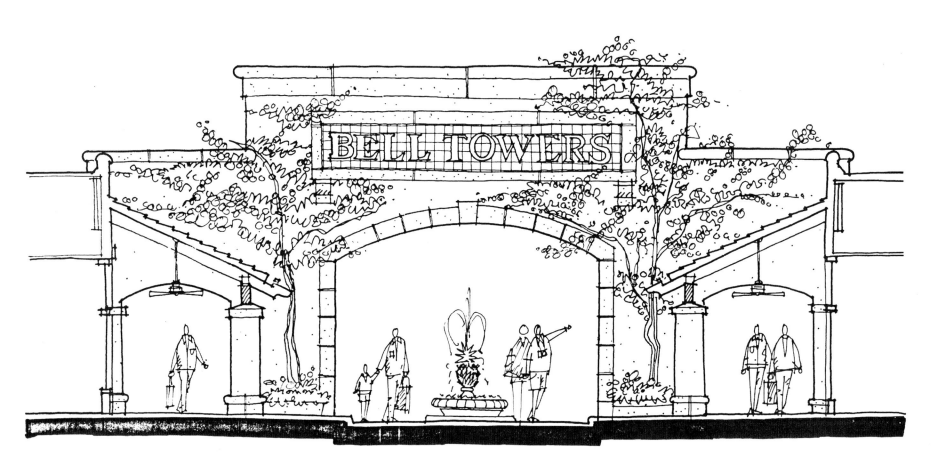

Drawing type: Elevation
Subject: Interior court
Medium/techniques: Hand drawn
Source: D'Agostino Izzo Quirk Architects

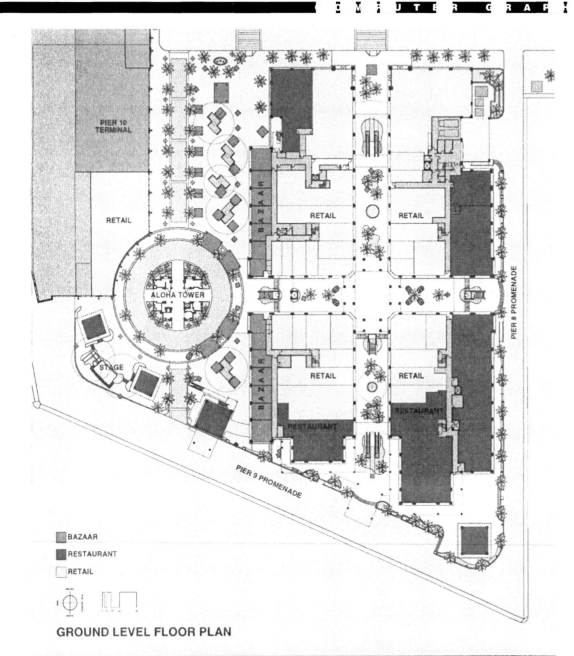

PIER 10
TERMINAL

RETAIL

BAZAAR

RETAIL

RETAIL

ALOHA TOWER

STAGE

BAZAAR

RETAIL

RETAIL

RESTAURANT

RESTAURANT

PIER 8 PROMENADE

PIER 9 PROMENADE

Drawing type: Site plan
Subject: Waterfront detail
Medium/techniques: Mac-based computer graphic program
Source: D'Agostino Izzo Quirk Architects

BAZAAR

RESTAURANT

RETAIL

GROUND LEVEL FLOOR PLAN

THE WATERFRONT AT ALOHA TOWER
HONOLULU, HAWAII

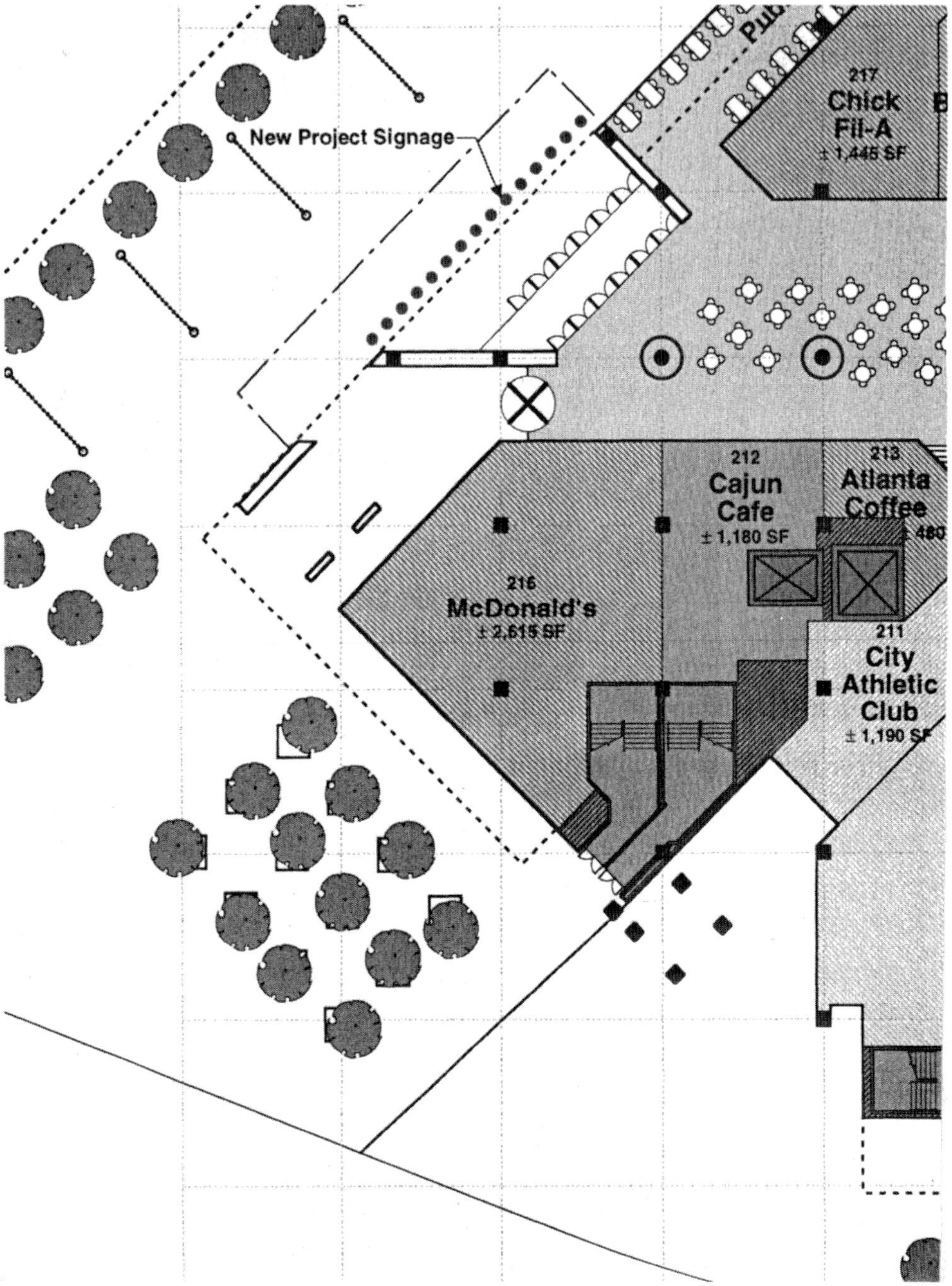

New Project Signage

217
Chick
Fil-A
± 1,445 SF

212
Cajun
Cafe
± 1,180 SF

213
Atlanta
Coffee
± 480

216
McDonald's
± 2,615 SF

211
City
Athletic
Club
± 1,190 SF

Drawing type: Floor plan
Subject: Shopping center
Medium/techniques: Mac-based computer graphic program
Source: D'Agostino Izzo Quirk Architects

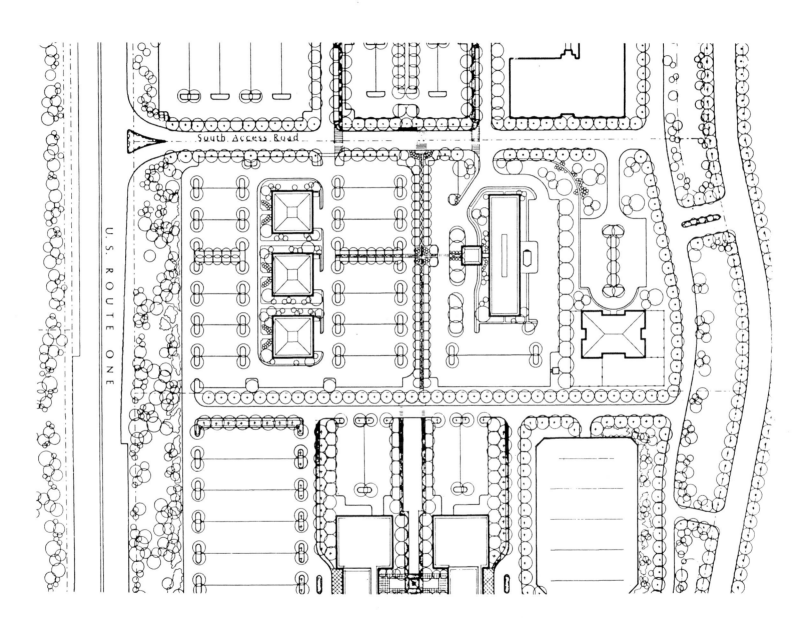

Drawing type: Site plan
Subject: Office complex
Medium/techniques: Autocad
Source: The Stubbins Associates Inc.